The X-Factor

The Spiritual Success Behind Successful Executives & Entrepreneurs

SOUL EXCELLENCE
PUBLISHING

Contents

Introduction

We are all addicted to the come down—to the fear, anxiety, and stress that keeps us on high alert.

As a fellow executive or entrepreneur, you may feel this in the dis-ease of Sunday evening when your mind is already racing through your to-do list for the week ahead. Your inability to stay in a "feel good" state may reveal itself when you shrug off a warranted compliment from a colleague. "It wasn't that great," you say. Or maybe you've recently earned a new title, hired an all-star team, and received a well-deserved bonus, and yet you think to yourself, *Something's got to give. This is too good to be true.*

These are common thoughts and experiences among our most competent, successful business leaders today. I know this because I talk to them day in and day out through my work as a publisher, author, speaker, and mentor to leaders in the corporate world. While we may be evolutionarily wired for fear, I believe we are in a moment in time where the future will be shaped by leaders who can shift out of fear and into love.

The Inspiration for This Book - And This Leadership Movement

Nestled in my comfy chair, looking out toward the city skyline, I thought this over and then asked, "What do people need to hear right now?" I took three deep breaths, pulled out my notebook and pen, and I wrote.

I had expected to write, think, and brainstorm for hours on the concept for the book that you now hold in your hands, for I felt that the world needed a great many things to heal at this moment in time.

But the concept came quickly out of my hand and onto the page.

Spirit. God. Love. Connection. Leadership. Freedom.

Within moments, in a spark of intuition and inspiration that I believe only happens when we are tapped into our soul and its abundant, ever-flowing love, the title came to me: *The X-Factor: The Spiritual Secrets Behind Successful Executives & Entrepreneurs.*

And just like that, I began to call in the business leaders who share this mission. The servant leaders, the faith-based executives, the men and women who understand that transformation must happen first from within to transform cultures, teams, organizations, and humanity. The leaders like *you* who recognize that there must be another way.

Spiritual Growth Calls for Human Relationships

As we collaborated in the creation of this book, I was involved in three experiences that challenged me to go deeper in my spiritual practices and to place more faith and trust in myself and God.

First, I joined an intimacy coaching program. Years ago on a retreat on lush Maui, I sat in a circle with other women, and we each shared what we desired most. Intimacy, I said automatically, not knowing where it came from within me. More recently as I tapped back into what I truly desire in life, the word *intimacy*, meaning *close-*

ness, reentered my consciousness. What I had yet to learn is that I had not given myself permission to fully see myself—to accept, love, and honor who God has called me to be.

Second, I participated in a six-month spiritual companioning program designed to help us bring heaven on earth in each and every moment. I had been drawn to the program's focus on the virtues as a tool for communication and connection. Over the course of the program, I began to realize how much time we spend on autopilot. Both our spiritual and material abundance is proportional to our ability to create space between stimulus and our response, our ability to be mindful, to align to our values, and to choose in each and every situation how we respond.

Finally, over the course of the creation of this book, I entered into a new romantic relationship, one of the best playgrounds for spiritual growth. I was given the opportunity to experience a new level of closeness and put my new awareness from intimacy coaching and the tools of spiritual companioning to the test as I navigated the big feelings associated with the relationship.

These experiences coalesced to remind and reveal to me the following:

1. Spiritual growth requires human relationships (and this book is calling you into a relationship with us, the authors).

2. The body and our feelings support our spiritual expansion (and give you guidance on whether you are on the path in each moment).

3. Spiritual leaders will lead us into the future (and they will exist in all fields at all levels).

The Spiritual Nature of Intimacy

My soul has always longed for intimacy. Has yours? Once I settled enough to recognize that it wasn't more best-sellers, more revenue, or a larger team that I desired, but rather, intimacy, God brought me a guide to help me experience just that.

I met Melisa Keenan, the founder of an international intimacy coaching business, on a women's business retreat held in Sedona, Arizona. As I navigated my new relationship and expanded my vision for this company heading into year two, Melisa was my rock. She was the person I turned to for daily guidance on how to understand what I was feeling and navigate difficult conversations. She never told me the answers. Instead she always invited me to drop in, to access my intuition, to listen to my soul. Her methods connected with me. Sometimes she would play a song to ground our call. Other times, she would invite me to visit my inner child, six-year-old Kayleigh. Every time, I felt more deeply connected to my true nature, seeing into me first, so I could see deeply into the souls of others.

You Are Not of This World

One day as we sat together on video in meditation, I heard it. "You are mine." It was Jesus. I grew up a practicing Catholic, and as I've explored and incorporated other spiritual practices, my Christian faith has only grown in its depth. As we explored a difficult situation in my life together, Jesus came to me with the most potent of reminders: "You are mine." I exhaled as the vision of Him and these words connected to my heart. I am His. This means that I am not the world's. I am not my critics'. I am not even bound to my thoughts or feelings. I am His. It was such a relief. A calling to embrace my true nature and to live courageously out in the world.

Do you feel this, too? Does it give you comfort and courage to live so open-heartedly?

The Body as Our Spiritual Guidance System

My work with Melisa also revealed that so much intelligence is contained within the body. For the first time, I began to practice tuning into my feelings at a body level, not at a mental one. This meant sitting for a moment and having her guide me to explore the following:

- How am I feeling?

- Where am I feeling this in my body?

- What does it feel like?

Most of the words I used to describe my feelings early on, I came to learn, were evaluations and judgments rather than unfiltered feelings. Over the course of three months, I began to experience what it meant to allow myself to have feelings and their role as my spiritual guidance system. They are a way to access deeper levels of our spirit; a way to sense what's going on in our world without the judgment, noise, or chatter of our egoic minds.

When we ponder things of the spirit, we often look up to the heavens. What I've learned is that I can observe feelings in my body, use them as indicators for action, and then make a choice to access heaven on earth right here, right now. The gift in this is that we don't have to wait another moment to connect with our spiritual selves and make choices from a place of true freedom.

Spiritual Companioning and the Gift of The Virtues

Over the summer of 2021, I also participated in a spiritual companioning mentorship group led by Tamala Ridge, a renowned addiction specialist living in Denmark, Australia, whom I had gotten to know the year before during a physical and spiritual detox experience she led that had served as a catalyst for going "all-in" on Soul Excellence.

I wanted to join the program because I knew that I had a desire to facilitate corporate retreats and felt that I could bring a new energy to the experience by having a set of spiritual tools to use. Again, I articulated a desire—how can I help leaders connect to spirit, God, and themselves during our work together?—and God brought a person into my life.

What desires are you not sharing? Who might be waiting in the wings to support you?

The Virtues as Our Connection Point to God

One of my favorite tools that Tamala introduced to me is the virtues
—that is, the character traits that exhibit moral excellence. The
Virtues Project looked across all cultures and religions to map out
the one hundred virtues that are at the heart of the human experience no matter where we are born or how we have been raised.
Their list of one hundred virtues has inspired me on so many levels.

I believe that the virtues are "the x-factor" when it comes to leadership communication today. They are the reminder to shift out of
opinion and into curiosity. Here are three simple ways that you can
use the virtues in your own personal and professional lives:

1. Pick a virtue each day to embody. Every day, I pull a card
from my deck of one hundred virtues. They sit on my desk held
together by a beautiful silver yogic statue. This past week, for example, I pulled the virtues of Openness, Fortitude, Sincerity, Trust, and
Forgiveness. Simply reading a card, I feel my spirit expand and
honor the fact that each of these virtues live within me, waiting to
be called upon. You can also search for and download the Virtues
Cards app to have them with you at all times.

2. Use virtues to infuse your communication. I am an opin-
ionated person. Don't we all feel encouraged to have strong opinions
these days? Yet opinions are not particularly helpful to our spiritual
expansion on earth because they box us in and force us to double
down and ignore new information and insight. The virtues have
helped me to infuse my communication with perspectives, not opinions. They invite curiosity and softness. They encourage me to hold
things lightly and express from my heart. Before you write an important email, communicate at a quarterly meeting, or speak to a
customer, pull a virtue to kick in the spiritual side of your being and
communicate from that more expansive place.

3. Invite your teams to reflect on the virtues. This is my
favorite. As I have led multiple groups of leaders to create these
powerful leadership books, I've used the virtues in our group calls as

a point of reflection and connection, and you can, too. Simply take ten minutes at the start of your next team meeting to share a virtue with your team and invite them to share their reflections on it. You will be blown away by what a simple word will spark in individuals! This shift in perspective is profound because the virtues bring in wonder, gratitude, and curiosity—the critical ingredients to innovation, communication, and collaboration.

Relationship as Spiritual Playgrounds

Finally, while we wrote this book, I came face-to-face with my own integrity and alignment. As we started the project, I met a radiant woman who shifted my reality. In fact, I wrote the following in my journal when we first met:

"Life can change in a moment. My life has changed this week. The trajectory will never be the same."

Our relationship blossomed as we enjoyed time at the beach, traded ideas about the future, and celebrated the fact that we had found each other! Suddenly, everything in my life—past relationships, heartbreaks, cross-country moves—made sense. I was made for this moment. I was made to love this person.

And then, I made a horrible mistake. Which I then followed up with a lie out of fear of losing her. The betrayal burned in my body; there was no way I could let it fester there for the lifetime that I wanted us to be together. After taking a moment for self-compassion —to really believe that I was not a horrible person but that I had made multiple mistakes—and accepting the fact that I had to have this difficult conversation even though I knew it would cost me the relationship, I made the dreaded call.

It was fairly straightforward, and the relationship was over on the spot. A decade ago, a mistake of this magnitude would have set me off into a downward spiral of self-loathing. *You are wrong! You are a horrible person! You should just hide for a while!* Today, thanks to my spiritual practices, I have the perspective to connect to my inner child, to have compassion for myself, to trust that I am worthy, whole, and loved. And to move forward gently, gently, slowly, slowly.

Still, I was left to wonder how I could destroy something so special. And the answers were clear: I had hit an upper limit, and I had abandoned my own spiritual practices.

Savoring Love Instead of Manufacturing Fear

The concept of upper limits was first put forth and described in the book *The Big Leap: Conquer Your Hidden Fear and Take Life to the Next Level* by NYT Bestseller, Gay Hendricks. Hendricks describes the problem like this:

> I have a limited tolerance for feeling good. When I hit my Upper Limit, I manufacture thoughts that make me feel bad….When I hit my Upper Limit, I do something that stops my positive forward trajectory… I do something that brings me back down within the bounds of my limited tolerance. (Hendricks, p. 7)

Everything in my life was going amazingly well, and I was living well above my average-set thermostat for feeling "good" and connected to self, others, God, and nature. And I subconsciously created a serious personal drama to bring me out of heaven and back down onto earth, although it felt more like hell.

I had also abandoned the very practices that had made it possible to reach a new echelon of success, joy, inspiration, and love. I went to my first twelve-step meeting at age twenty-five while living in Washington, DC. I hadn't hit rock bottom, but I felt the daily pain and discomfort of living two lives—one where I was connected, sober, and free, and the other where I was anxious, disconnected, and a slave to impulse.

After five years of living sober and fully alive, I thought I had it under control. I thought that the last few years of occasional drinking were just fine. It was fun, after all, to sip wine by the lake at Gundlach Bundschu in Sonoma. I loved popping champagne when we hit bestseller status with our first two multi-author leadership books. Little did I realize that I was playing with fire, that I was one drink away from burning down my own house. But play with fire I did.

And so as we go to publish this book, I am being called back into the highest version of integrity, which means living in alignment with my personal values. It means that the spiritual connection is the priority; it is foundational, not tangential. I believe that this book is divinely timed. For me, it represents a coming home, a return to the truth of who I am, who God created me to be. It represents a step on the path of the highest integrity. There is no variance or wiggle room now for how I must live. The call is for total alignment, and when I am out of alignment, to return as quickly as possible.

As of writing this introduction, there is hope to rebuild the relationship. I consider this a gift of the spiritual journey that I've been on. I can sit in the unknown, hold space for a loved one, and not beat myself up—these are spiritual gifts.

The X-Factor Is Spiritual Connection

What is my final spiritual secret to offer you along with the other authors in this book?

Create the space for the spirit to reach you through other people.

Spiritual growth cannot truly take hold unless we share growth with a community. This book is your invitation to walk with us on this leadership and spiritual journey. The leaders who share their stories in this anthology come from all over the world and have led various teams and companies. They share their stories openly in this book in order to embody what it means to walk the spiritual path. There are times when the path requires solitude and a solo pilgrim's journey. And then there are moments, like now, where the path requires vulnerability, openness, and connection. As you read their stories, open your heart to receive what is meant for you at this moment in your journey.

Don't Be Shy; Connect with the Authors in This Book

I encourage you to reach out to the authors whose stories resonate with your heart. Connect with them on LinkedIn or send them an email. There is so much beauty and growth in dialogue. I also encourage you to share this book with fellow leaders. Let's start this movement together. Let's awaken those who are ready to receive the messages contained within this book so that they feel supported and emboldened to bring a spiritual lens to their work, teams, companies, and society at large.

Thank you for walking this path. Take heart that you are right where you need to be, and trust that your deep connection to your spiritual self gives you choice and freedom. Your attention to your spiritual growth will make you a better leader because you will be open to receive ideas and create solutions with guidance from an intellectual force greater than yourself.

Lastly, I remind you that spiritual growth is not just about your connection to God or spirit or your fellow man. We are called to connect back to ourselves first and foremost in the moments when we feel feelings that we don't like, such as hurt, discomfort, or embarrassment. I leave you with one simple spiritual practice that I recently learned as a member of a Lindsey Schwartz's Powerhouse Women Mastermind. When you feel those negative emotions, connect to your spiritual self, by reciting the following:

I love you.
It's safe to feel this way.
You're welcome to stay here as long as you want.
I know you're for me.
I'll be right here, loving you.

Can you imagine what it would feel like to extend yourself this level of compassion during your darkest moments?

Can you imagine what would shift in your soul to trust that the right thing will come about without trying to make it happen?

Can you imagine how you would treat others if you loved yourself in this way?

This is the new path of leadership. This is spiritual leadership. This is Soul Excellence leadership.

Congratulations on picking up this book, on saying yes to the spiritual leadership journey, on *being* the leader called to transmute fear into love.

With love and hope,
Kayleigh O'Keefe
Founder, Soul Excellence Publishing

ONE

Sarah Alaimo

MY EVER-PROGRESSING DEFINITION OF SUCCESS

Our lives are what we make them…or something like that. In 2007, I began my career as a recruiter. I found my thing, my niche. I found success and notoriety, and my first professional year set forth impossible expectations. *Of course, I will continue to be promoted and get $10,000 raises; this is just how things are going to be for me,* I thought.

Sarah Alaimo, SHRM-CP, CCHC, *Pearls and Probation: Adventures of an Alcoholic Good Girl*

I am an entrepreneur. I am a leader. I am a mentor. I am a daughter, sister, wife, and friend. As such, I am not terminally unique. I suffer from the same human condition that you do. The difference —or quite possibly another similarity that ties us together—is that for years I tried to work my way quite literally through and over basic human traits and characteristics. Being driven by a definition of success and life goals ingrained into my psyche since birth, I had certain expectations for myself and the world as I entered the coveted "real world," and initially, I was far too motivated and ambitious to make any concessions.

Twenty-one-year-old Sarah would define success quite differently than present-day Sarah. The fresh faced, naïve, hopeful, and eager woman who graduated from Seattle Pacific University with a degree in communication and minors in business and economics had a vision of what success should look like. Success results in financial security, stability, a beautiful home, nice cars, travel, and a sense of ease and comfort. Young Sarah knew that success included hard work and would require maintaining a certain standard of work. This was not something that she was afraid of. Not in the least. In fact, she could not be more excited to graduate and hit the ground running so that she could get started on her own grown-up, professional, corporate success.

Present day, I have achieved many levels of success throughout my career—throughout my life, for that matter! There was success right off the bat in my first career position where I was promoted and given a substantial raise within the first six months. This, unfortunately, set the stage for some very unrealistic expectations moving forward. Titles were king—or queen, rather—and there were very blurred lines between updating LinkedIn to announce a promotion and actual wholeness, happiness, or fulfillment.

Financial freedom was always a factor. Whether I was making good money or not, money was always a factor. I do not know the magic number I was working so hard to achieve, but I can say that it was a moving target that I was not sure I was ever going to hit!

New roles, new companies, and promotions led to increased responsibility. That was the world in which I had learned to thrive! Over the years that "all or nothing" and "more is better" mentality slowly crept up on me. The vision of the innocent, bright-eyed new college grad ready to take on the world became a mere memory. In her place stood a woman who was lost, tired, and hiding from her Higher Power. But no one on the outside could see that woman on the inside. What they saw was a coordinated, organized leader with a smile on her face.

Grace Called on August 23, 2015

I woke up in a hospital on a bed that was being moved from a dark hallway into a very bright space with white curtains dividing up the cold, sterile room. I could not sort out where I was on my own. I was finally told that I was in the emergency room at Harborview Medical Center, dizzy as a duck and wanting to know what was going on. The words coming out of my mouth were slow and hard to push out. Once out of my mouth, they felt fat and swollen and sounded funny.

I put my left hand on the back of my head, and it felt gooey. I brought my hand back in front of my face to investigate, and it was covered in blood. I tried to alert the nurse who had her back turned to me that something was wrong, and she assured me she was aware that my head was open and bleeding. I was told that I just had a CT scan, and they were awaiting the results or something like that. I have no idea how long we were there. I have no idea how long they waited for my blood alcohol level to go down enough to put nine staples in my head.

I could not say when my sister arrived. I don't know how long she and her fiancée stayed. But I knew she was angry with me for nearly dying. She shared with me that the doctor told her I should have died from my fall off of the houseboat onto the concrete dock below. That my 3.9 blood alcohol level should have killed me if the concussion that resulted from the fall didn't. She shared with me that a 4.0 blood alcohol level typically results in certain death. Then she left. She was too angry to be around me.

I was discharged that night. I was reeling, tired, in pain, confused, hopped up on some sort of pain meds they gave me when they put the staples in, and still wearing my pink, two-piece swimsuit from the party the previous day. Luckily, the friend I went to the party with never left my side. He got us an Uber, and we made our way back to my house, where I simply got into bed and had the deepest sleep of my life.

When I woke up the next morning, all I knew was that I did not ever have to drink again. I hadn't wanted to for a very long time, but at this point, not only did I no longer *want* to, but I also no longer *had* to. And so, the recovery journey began, then and there. That morning was my spiritual experience that changed my life forever.

Spiritual Awakening

Years earlier, in college, one of my professors spoke about the difference between vocation and avocation. The majority of us know what a vocation is—our principal occupation. Some may go so far as to refer to this as one's calling, and others may say this is simply the tasks that pay the bills. Conversely, avocation is more like a hobby or work done outside of a typical 8:00–5:00 job. An avocation is often referred to as one's "true" passion or interest. Do the two ever coincide? Can your vocation be your avocation? Or can your avocation bring in the Benjamins to pay the bills like other vocations?

Enter career happiness coaching. Our occupation, job, or employment doesn't always have to be the naysayer in the back of our minds stealing our joy. Once I learned this, there was no holding me back! I honestly thought it was a myth that more than a few professionals would refer to their 8:00–5:00, Monday through Friday commitment as their calling, mission, or even purpose. And once I honed in on the things that get me out of bed in the morning—helping others—I, too, was able to find the connective thread holding the words "career" and "happiness" together. Now this next part will blow your mind. Once I discovered my career happiness, I began to feel (that darn four-letter F word) all of the feelings—good, bad, or indifferent—in my daily work. I began to hone in on what parts of my work were the best parts of my day.

While that professional transformation was taking place, I was also on a personal journey. My journey into and through recovery as a way of life. Recovery from alcohol addiction, perfectionism, imposter syndrome, anxiety, and critical self-talk. Along with this new way of doing life, it was the perfect time to take a chance on myself and explore this newfound freedom.

Career Happiness Coaching

Fulfillment is the achievement of a desire, promise, or prediction. How do we find that feeling or define that truth for ourselves? Happiness cannot truly be measured by any hard facts or metrics. Of course, there are indirect results of happiness, such as employee engagement or retention. Happiness is an emotion or feeling of joy, satisfaction, contentment, and fulfillment.

My vocabulary has changed over the past six years. Realization of the true meaning of achievement, satisfaction, and accomplishment and what it took to attain that state of freedom began to form. In its purest form, achievement refers to something done successfully, typically by effort, courage, or God-given skill. Satisfaction is the fulfillment of one's wishes, expectations, or needs. Or even the next level of one deriving pleasure as a result of this fulfilled goal. An accomplishment is the successful achievement of a task. Typically, this is seen as an activity that one can do well in as a result of study or practice.

Success is often viewed as the opposite of failure. The criterion for success depends on the context and varies based on one's belief system. The cultural norm of success being the attainment of wealth, prosperity, or fame fueled my drive for many years. In really looking into the word and its meanings globally, I came across a definition I could really get behind: the desired result of an attempt; less stressful yet, meeting one's obligations and the fulfillment of their basic needs; and the ability to identify absolute needs versus wants.

Simplicity always seemed synonymous with laziness or lacking intelligence in my idealistic mind. I certainly sought a life of simplicity, but still a big life, a fun life, an impactful life—so never the twain shall meet. Right? Wrong! For years the word "balance" was my

North Star. The goal. The dream. The word pasted all over every vision board I started but never completed. My coach, Carol, always says that the elusive hunt for "work–life balance" is in and of itself an unproductive goal. It insinuates that our work is not a part of our life. Or that our life does not include our work. In all reality, it is one and the same.

Whether you work to live or live to work, what is really important?

The X-Factor

For me, Sarah Alaimo of Redmond Washington, the X-Factor is faith, and literally or figuratively, turning my will over to the care of God, as I understand Him.

Does success equal happiness? I have never been very good at math —a fact I want to stop telling myself—but I do believe that statement is not correct. The achievement of goals? Having a place to call home? Belief in myself and accepting the knowledge that I am doing exactly what I am supposed to be doing? Have you ever heard the saying, "I can't. God can. I think I will let Him"?

After so many years of feigning happiness, I wasn't sure how to know when I truly was happy. Well, I will tell you that you will know when you are. Happiness, for me, is feeling that the conditions of my life are good and that more often than not I am living with positive feelings and feeling hopeful and accomplished.

This is not to say that my life is perfect. Of course, there is sunshine and the occasional rainbow, but there is also hard work, sacrifice, and growth. All of which can be very uncomfortable. Especially for someone who sought not to feel anything for years. I have learned to feel my way through the discomfort. I have learned to pray for my attention to be directed away from myself and toward others. I have learned that I get so much more than I give when I help others. In the past I would have chosen words like joy, excitement, and overall contentment to describe what happiness means to me. What I have learned in my recovery journey is that gratitude, pride, and optimism fall into the same category.

Another key to success and overall satisfaction with life that I have learned through this journey is that this one word is a complete sentence—are you ready for it? No. Is your mind blown? Now, we can politely decline or even choose to not reply in cases where the ask could be for volunteers and such. But I have discovered that it is 100 percent totally and fully okay to say no to a request. And it doesn't matter what the request is for. I have even gone so far as to say, "I am not available for X, Y, and Z." The extra insane part of this discovery is that, more often than not, the individual I am saying this to is not personally offended by my response and, usually, is not waiting for a long, drawn-out explanation to my answer.

For the entirety of my years leading up to my early thirties, I probably declined a request, suggestion, or demand fewer times than I am comfortable estimating. For some reason, I had it engrained in my brain that through works and an overall compliant nature, I could eventually achieve success, forget about worry, and find true happiness.

So, here is the big secret! I found those things when I stopped overthinking it all. I literally stopped sweating the small stuff. And I turned over the really important things to God. When I was able to do this, my life became easier and bigger things began to happen. Larger dreams than the ones I had for myself.

Today when I coach clients, interview a potential employee, or chat with a mentee, I have learned to listen far more than I speak. Through my own journey, I have learned that we all *know* our own truths deep down inside. I just needed someone else's voice asking me the important questions. There is not a global secret to life or success. Your individualized secret recipe is within you. I am grateful for the fateful day that set me on the journey to discover that recipe. I am also thankful for the drive to continue to grow on that journey. The journey makes me grow as a human, and the amazing sideeffects are improved communication, a larger and more positive outlook on everything, and the ability to lead others with a heart of servant leadership.

The Test

Don't worry, this test is not timed and will not be any portion of your grade. In fact, only you know the answers to these questions. How do you measure happiness? What does the word success mean to you today? Has your picture of success changed over the years? Did an event or string of life events contribute to that change of view? Does your life today resemble your image of success? If so, is there anything you do daily to nurture and grow in that space? If not, what is one thing you can do today to start moving your life in that direction?

Okay, thank you for your participation in that brief, but incredibly insightful game of twenty questions. If any of those questions were difficult, I challenge you to take a little time to think about them. Maybe put pen to paper. I have found when I do that, I learn an awful lot about myself.

If those questions were easy and you have all of the answers, may I ask one more question? What do you want to do when you grow up? Are you doing it? Is it something you have been putting off for years? Well, today is a great day to make a start! Having this vision is the first step in my coaching process with clients. Sometimes the goals change along the way, but that is just a part of the overall process.

My journey to a life run on faith rather than fear was a longer, bumpier road than I originally anticipated. I never thought I could honestly say that it was all worth it, but today I do believe those words. Along the way I learned a lot and am able to pass that along to my clients today. For the journey, the gifts, and the blessings, I am incredibly grateful.

With thanks,
Sarah

About the Author

SARAH ALAIMO

Sarah Alaimo is a career happiness coach specializing in serving women in recovery. Sarah is also an Amazon bestselling author, healthcare recruitment leader, and recovery advocate. A Southern California native massively deprived of sunshine while living in the Pacific Northwest, Sarah loves her black Pomeranian, Baron, ice cream, the Los Angeles Angels of Anaheim baseball, travel adventures, and her husband, John. While she would love to say that she has learned moderation since getting sober in 2015, the fact that she listed ice cream before her husband really says it all.

LinkedIn:
www.linkedin.com/in/sarahdalaimo
Website: www.sarahalaimo.com
Contact: 206.963.8850 & hello@sarahalaimo.com
Author page:
https://www.amazon.com/kindle-dbs/sarahalaimo

Books:
Pearls & Probation: Adventures of an Alcoholic Good Girl.
The Good Girl's Guide to Career Happiness: 6 Simple Steps to Professional Fulfillment (January 2022 release).

TWO

Karen Ann Bulluck

OF BOXES AND BOUNDARIES: HOW MY SPIRITUAL JOURNEY TAUGHT ME TO BREAK FREE OF BOXES AND LIVE WITHIN BOUNDARIES

I grew up in boxes, not literally, of course, but in a world with a lot of rules, regulations, and expectations. I know I'm not unusual in that, although my parents and grandmothers were on the rigid side of the scale.

Boxes are often how we keep ourselves safe. They are how we make sense of the world. It's perfectly normal human behavior to define and categorize the things and people in our world so that we can understand, relate to others appropriately and meaningfully, and know what is and isn't dangerous to us. It's how we survive, and it's how we've succeeded as a species.

But you know all that. So, what's the problem with boxes? Well, in addition to helping us feel safe and understand our world, they can also keep us very, very small. For instance, when I applied for my first corporate job as a trainer, my father told me that it was a job that I didn't want to do. Why? Because in his mind, I didn't fit into the box where I had to stand up in front of people and talk. If I had listened to him and stayed in *his* box for me, I would never have taken that job, and it was absolutely the right job for me at the time.

My spirituality in particular was a place where I experienced a lot of boxes. As a child, my spiritual understanding was all about mainstream Protestant values and beliefs. There were the rules and commandments that we usually learned at church, not necessarily bad ones, but a lot of them. God (please feel free to substitute your preferred name for the divine impulse in the world) was less of a mystery and a creator than the keeper of the commandments and the rules that one had to follow to both succeed at life and go to heaven at death. But despite this sometimes harsh view of God, church and mainstream Christianity still pulled me in. There was a beauty in the rules, but also in the music, the rituals, the sense of belonging to something bigger. I was very devout and devoted to the rules, maybe a little too much so. However, they did keep me out of trouble in my teenage years.

What I didn't understand as a child, and what took me years to grow into, was the concept of boundaries. Boxes were clearly defined, rigid, and consistent in their shape and structure. There were either boxes or nothing. I hadn't really experienced the option of fluid, flexible, yet firm boundaries that would keep me safe but not small. Flexible boundaries were not part of my religious experience nor my home life. So, all I could see at the beginning was boxes, and eventually, they grew too restrictive, too tiresome, and altogether too uncomfortable. I wanted desperately to escape, but to what?

The First Glimpses of Freedom

In my first semester in college, I made the mistake (maybe) of taking a course that essentially examined all the literature that said God was a myth. Yes, Nietzsche's famous quote, "God is dead," was on the reading list. The course material played into all the doubts, questions, and concerns I had secretly held even during my most devout periods as a child. Suddenly, the world shifted, and I was freed from the box of religion. But I lost a loving God and my sense of the divine too, or I tried to. After all, what good is not having the box of religious rules and expectations when you still feel guilty or accountable to a higher power?

Does that mean that I went wild? Sadly, no, although it might have been better for me if I had. After all, college provides a relatively safe environment for young people to explore the limits of their boundaries. But the boxes and rules that had governed my life continued to do so. Yes, I had many more doubts, more little rebellions, and attended church a lot less, but the course of my life didn't change. I even insisted that my first husband and I get married in a church. The heart of my spiritual beliefs held, as it has all my life.

When my career path expanded and changed in my late twenties, my life started looking a lot different. Things that had fit neatly in boxes before started to feel very small and unsatisfying. The world outside the boxes looked big and pretty and FREE! I was finally at a point, with more financial freedom and the confidence of success at work, where I really started breaking down the boxes. And yeah, things started to go a little wild then.

One of the spiritual secrets behind my early success, well, really all of it, was the good old Protestant work ethic. I know that work ethic is considered obsolete these days in some circles, but putting in a hard day's work is always a good step in the direction of success. That set of rules did serve me well, even when things outside of the office went a little wonky. I could always fall back on that ethic, that sense of responsibility to get my work done and get it done well. Although I didn't know it at the time, I was starting to see where boundaries were needed in my life. The work ethic wasn't a box; it was a boundary and a good one.

As I explored my newfound freedom, I found myself once again rejecting the rigid structure of the religion of my youth and exploring other spiritual avenues. At that time, the New Age movement was very appealing with its lack of rules, belief in the benevolent universe, and roots in positive thinking and manifestation. I read a lot of what to me were alternative spiritual texts (Deepak Chopra, for example). I went to crystal shops and psychics with my friends. And while it all seemed happy and supportive and expansive, I couldn't quite get my head around the lack of rules. Oh, I enjoyed breaking a lot of the rules that I had always followed, but there was still something uncomfortable about right and wrong being so subjective.

And then things went a bit off track. My husband calls my thirties my postponed adolescence. In a way, he's right. I was pretty buttoned up in my teenage years, so my true rebellion came later in life. I think most of us eventually find a way to break out, and that happens at different places in everyone's lives. Anyway, my thirties were a blur of fun, exploration, and testing the limits of my freedom in sometimes extreme ways (like turning airplanes upside down), except at work, where that good old work ethic served me in good stead. But even there I was pushing out of the boxes and limits of the early part of my career and trying on new roles and new responsibilities, even if they were sometimes a bit more than I could handle as well as I would have liked. I was breaking free of boxes, but I was also ignoring important boundaries. The ones that kept me safe and making good decisions.

Like many people in rebellion, I made some decisions that were not in my best interest or the best interest of other people in my life. I eventually found myself in a bad relationship and realized that my disregard for some boundaries had gotten me further off track than I would have liked. I needed to reassess where I was and where I was going, especially on my spiritual path, because I wanted to make changes, and I needed some support to do that.

Maybe the Boxes Aren't So Bad

I turned back to church. I guess when we're really in a hard place, we often go back to what we know, where we've found comfort in the past. In this case, it was an incredible blessing. The pastor of the local Presbyterian church was an older woman who came to ministry later in life. She was wise, caring, and not at all rigid. She gave me hope that I could recover and reset. She helped me start to trust in God again. With her guidance and a great deal of prayer, I had an experience with Jesus that gave me the courage and strength to get out of the bad relationship and to draw new boundaries in my life. It shifted me back onto a safer path.

And that's when—with the help of the pastor—I started to understand that maybe some of the rules that I had seen as a box were truly boundaries to keep me safe. I also started to understand that maybe God was bigger and more spacious than the role She had been assigned by the constructs of human institutions. It was the start of a big shift in my thinking. While boxes are restrictive, could boundaries keep me safe and provide a foundation in which I could truly find freedom? It was a lot to get my head around, but it was the start of a whole new phase of my life and my spiritual growth.

It was about this time that I got my first full executive title. I was promoted to a vice president role. I began looking harder at the bigger picture at work, as well as the bigger picture of my life. My new grounding in faith based on a relationship with the divine rather than all those rules supported my confidence. My new experience with boundaries helped me start to keep toxic things and people out of my life. I started trusting more in my higher self, my intuition, and had a bigger sense of the sacred in all aspects of my life. And it wasn't too long after all of this that I met my current husband—at church, of course.

Educations in Ethics and Energy

As my career progressed, my boss encouraged me to go back to school to get a graduate-level degree. He didn't think an MBA was the right fit for me and encouraged me to look around to find a master's program that would interest me and help me grow. I found myself drawn to organizational leadership programs that focused on people and processes. Several programs intrigued me, but the one at Regis University in Denver, Colorado, held the most appeal. Regis is a smallish Jesuit college and is regionally recognized in the west. They have a solid and successful online program with industry-experienced professors. The biggest draw for me, however, was the capstone course or thesis. It was called Ethical Decision-Making. Now there was something that I wanted to explore. I loved that the program was ethically and, on a subtle level, spiritually driven. I was making more and more decisions with an overt eye on how they would impact both my spiritual growth and my integrity.

As I suspected, the capstone project on Ethical Decision-Making had a profound impact on me. Not only did I learn a variety of decision-making skills, some that I use with clients in my coaching practice today, but I also learned a lot about myself and my boundaries around integrity. The final project involved recommending a course of action based on a case study. The study I chose was one where a young woman was being asked to do something unethical in her work. It wasn't exactly illegal, but in my view, the request bordered on it. My conclusion was that she should leave the job, even if it meant taking a financial setback. It helped me define a clear boundary that my integrity was more important than money, a boundary that continues to be a foundation for my life and my work.

Translating my studies to the working environment, I took a more active role in building relationships throughout the organization, even with people who were often on the opposite side of the internal battles for resources and strategy. When my role expanded to a senior vice president level and a much larger team, these relationships became a key part of my strategy to build understanding, cooperation, and—as much as possible—consensus between the company's various division leaders. Approaching everyone with a view of myself and them as spiritual and divinely created beings gave me a sense of compassion and hope. Did these relationships always go the way I wanted them to? Of course not, but I was able to put some of my own competitiveness and ambition aside for the greater good more than I think I would have had I not had the expansive spiritual underpinning to my life.

During this time, my spiritual journey was also evolving. I loved so much of traditional Christianity, but it always troubled me that God would exclude people just because they weren't Christian. I didn't give up on it entirely. It's still a big part of who I am and how I relate to God, but I felt that the religion itself was defining the divine in a way that was too small for my growing understanding of God. I started exploring again, wanting to see how other faiths and other people understood and related to the divine. I also wanted to see where the valuable boundaries, hidden in religious rules, overlapped and were repeated. I found so much beauty and wisdom in religious and spiritual writings and teachings from all over the world. These studies helped increase my compassion and tolerance for people of all faiths and backgrounds and spiritual journeys. I recognized that there is not one clearly defined path to follow. We all have to find the narrow and winding path where Spirit leads each of us.

In the meantime, my career continued to grow. It was clear that my boss was grooming me to take over his job when he retired. Although that wasn't close, it wasn't too far from the horizon. I enjoyed the challenges, but there was something else gnawing at me. It went back to the reason I chose the master's program that I did. I was more interested in the people, in the interpersonal dynamics, than I often was in the mechanics of the business. I was starting to sense that I didn't really want to inherit my boss's job, that there was something else for me. In hindsight, I think it was a nudge from my higher self.

So, I went to a career coach, which led me to get my own coaching certification. Of course, that program also has strong spiritual overtones. It's not religious or explicitly spiritual, but the foundational principle is energy. Through what kind of energetic lens are we seeing the world? What kind of energy are we bringing into the world? How connected are we to each other? I learned so much about myself and others in that program. I felt so much better equipped for my job. Using what I learned as a coach as part of my executive function made a huge difference in relating to people. I could recognize the type of energy people were bringing to work and try to help shift that energy where possible. I loved that at work, and I love it now with my clients. When our energy level is high, when we are connected to divine energy or our higher selves, solutions are so much easier to find and so much more creative and expansive than when we are mired in negative energy.

Stepping Outside the Corporate Box

When I finally decided to leave the corporate world and strike out on my own, it was my spiritual journey that paved the way. After going on a retreat (okay, more than one) in Maui, my energy and enthusiasm for life outside of the corporate box were overflowing. I had been experiencing the symptoms of inner conflict, of misalignment with my higher self—the lethargy, lack of enthusiasm, crankiness, and fatigue that show us so clearly when we are out of alignment with ourselves. I felt that I was being called to using my coaching skills and experience in new ways, with different people.

Before I left, I did begin challenging the boxes there with varying degrees of success, and I made enough progress that I saw real opportunities for other people to start breaking down those corporate boxes and power-over behavior that are such an energy drain in many organizations. It gave me hope and excitement that I could help other people do the same thing in their organizations. During my corporate career, I had challenged the status quo, broken barriers, and supported new processes and practices that empowered people to grow and succeed. And I didn't want to stop that, I just wanted to do it in a different way.

Still, the decision was a huge step outside the boxes that I had been in for a long time. I think the ultimate factor was the one that was solidified during my master's program. I felt like I couldn't keep doing what I was doing and maintain my integrity. It wasn't outer integrity, like in the case study, but it was my internal integrity, my own peace of mind. I had to follow the path where I was being led, being called.

I want to put an important asterisk on this decision. I don't think the answer for everyone is "leaving corporate", although I know a lot of

people who feel that way these days. (It's something that corporations worldwide should be paying attention to.) There are ways to be
in the corporate world and still maintain your integrity. It's a matter
of really tuning into and listening to your higher self, to that part of
you that connects with the divine and enables you to see beyond the
day-to-day struggles and conflicts of corporate life. There are also
plenty of companies that treat employees with respect and have an
eye on more than just the bottom line.

Yes, corporations have to make money. That is why they exist, and
there's nothing inherently wrong with that. Companies just go about
it in different ways. When I've worked with clients and co-workers,
we often find that leaving corporate doesn't make sense and isn't
what they truly want. But what usually does make sense is setting
boundaries, listening to their inner wisdom, and reclaiming a sense
of integrity and alignment with their values. Oh, that's not always
easy, but there are strategies that can help people improve their work
situations, even if it's only while they look for a job where the
company's culture and values are more aligned with their own.

My Journey Now

For myself, I am finding a great deal of freedom in both setting
boundaries and breaking out of more old boxes in my life now. I am
able to set boundaries around my work schedule so that I can take
better care of my health: exercising more and eating better. At the
same time, I am breaking down boxes that I've put myself in
because of my very introverted nature. I am writing chapters in
books like this one. I self-published my first novel, *Ascending Ladders*. I
recently was a guest on my first podcast. I am co-hosting a monthly
roundtable on enlightened leadership for the women's networking
group LeadHership Global. I'm learning what I need to do to take
care of myself as I stretch my limits and put myself out in the world
in new ways. It's exciting and scary, and I'm grateful to have my
spiritual practices, my faith in God, and the support of my friends
and husband.

In the course of my spiritual journey, I've come to believe that God (the divine, the universe, or however you want to name the spiritual force in the world) is much bigger than we ever give Him credit for being. We limit God in our attempts to understand Her just like we limit each other (and ourselves) in our attempts to understand and control each other. We like to label things, and that's okay, as long as we remember that labels are only part of the picture, even labels we put on ourselves. I've also learned that there are universal boundaries built into the world's great religions that help us live healthier lives both on our own and in community. These are not boxes; they are boundaries that keep us safe. However, there are also boxes built into those same religions, into society, and into most human organizations that keep us small and controllable. True freedom comes from recognizing the difference, using boundaries to create a safe place to learn and grow, and breaking free of the boxes that keep us from reaching our full potential.

About the Author

KAREN ANN BULLUCK

Karen Ann Bulluck is a bestselling author, coach, and speaker. She was an executive vice president and member of the board of directors at AM Best Company, the insurance rating agency and information provider, before leaving to fulfill her dreams of writing and coaching.

In her chapter, Karen will reveal how her spiritual journey contributed to her success by expanding her perspective *and* learning to keep herself safe.

As a coach, Karen helps her clients develop an executive presence that is based on *their* core values and beliefs rather than the "expected" corporate image. She supports them in bringing their whole, authentic self to the workplace, reducing internal stress, improving relationships, and increasing creativity.

Karen is the author of the novel, *Ascending Ladders*, which follows a female executive as she brings her higher self to work. Karen is a contributing author to the book *Significant Women: Leaders Reveal What Matters Most*.

Karen holds a BA from the University of Virginia and an MS in organization leadership from Regis University, Denver, CO. She received her professional coach certification from iPEC. She lives in New Jersey with her husband and two very spoiled cats.

Website: www.higherselfsolutions.com
LinkedIn: https://www.linkedin.com/in/karenannbulluck/
Facebook: https://www.facebook.com/KarenAnnBulluck/
Email: karen@higherselfsolutions.com

THREE

Jaymie Scotto Cutaia

LETTER TO MY DAUGHTER

My Daughter Ava Capri,

As I write this, you are nestled in your crib, strong and wild, naturally confident. Nearly one year of age, you've already affected so much positive change, little one.

You've helped me see the world through a different lens, even at a time when the world stood still, with a pandemic spreading through the air, masking us all, locking us indoors, forcing us to vacate cities, trying to find a sense of cleanliness and renewal.

You, our miracle, came to us and taught us quickly that it's no longer about disruption, upheaval, net profits and losses or exit strategies. It's now about life, balance, purpose, impact, faith.

We as business leaders are considering the future. We are approaching a new time when we can reopen our doors yet keep this new sense of balance, this slowing down of time, this consideration of not just the 'how much' but the 'how' and the 'why', our true motivations.

I've begun writing this down for you, scraps of paper on my night table, this letter, to try to make sense of it as well.

We as humans are trying to escape from this place in history, escape from fear and ignorance. We are trying to govern ourselves with leadership and education; we are trying to act from the heart, guided by spirituality. There is so much confusion, pain, and hurt out there, that the water seems so murky. It's difficult to navigate.

So let's start with what I believe in. I believe God is everywhere. I see Him in the changing colors of the leaves on the trees, and when the wind plays with your sweet hair while you are sliding down the slide in the park.

I don't particularly subscribe to one religion. I don't look to other humans when I want to speak to God. I just pray, and miraculously, time after time, I feel heard and loved by Him. I am very spiritual, and I believe in the power of the spirit, both the divine spirit and the human spirit, and I believe that together, we can do great things and make the world better.

Everyone has their own beliefs, practices their own religions, reads their own books, gets their own news feeds. Nevertheless, I believe there's a clear, common thread throughout most of these belief systems and religions: to treat one another with respect and love.

The funny part about people is that we are more alike than we are different. We are more good than not. We all have a light inside of us, whether recognized or not.

I could feel your light even as early as the first weeks you lived inside me. Your soul is so present—its own living entity. With this amazing gift of you in our lives, I now fully believe in miracles and in a greater path forward. I fully believe in you, my little one. You, like faith, are a strong little mast standing tall against wind and waves.

If I was asked when was the one moment in my life I truly understood faith, truly felt God inside me, it would be when I felt you, my beautiful child, nestled and growing inside me. Truly, the world finally made sense to me.

My new greatest fear is that I won't be there, right when you really need me. So here are some lessons I have learned along the way that

I would like to pass down to you, as guidance for when you find yourself filled with more questions than answers.

1. You Are Stronger than You Realize. That flame inside of you will keep you pushing beyond what you may consider your limitations to be. Trust in it. Trust in yourself. I believe strength comes from the connection between your soul, your body, and your mind. There is energy from the connection of all three. Try to feel it; try to grow it; try to be nourished by it. Try to exercise it.

Caring for yourself is vital. Hearing yourself is vital. Trusting in yourself is vital. As you probably already know by the time you read this, I practice yoga as it's a great way to connect all three of your selves (body, spirit, mind) together in one meditation of movement. I'm sure you will find your own way of connecting, and feeling the power of that connection. Recognize that inside you is an undeniable energy, a force that can do great good.

2. Your Light Can Connect with Others. Like a candle flame that is joined with another, together people can cast a wider glow and create more of an impact against the darkness. You are made in God's light and likeness. Your light is God-like and can and should be used for greatness.

Do not be afraid to share your light. When you see someone who is in need, share your energy, pass it forward. You will notice you can raise someone just by injecting your light into their lives, even just by passing your energy to them or by listening to them.

Sometimes people just want to be heard. You can learn from each person, you just need to take the moment and share your light with him/her. Doing so will not deplete you; it will raise you up.

Together, people who feel your energy and understand you, and in turn, you understand them, can become an unmistakable force and, ideally, do a tremendous amount of good. If you want to move a mountain, employ amazing people you inspire with a singular purpose. Through the power of people, that mountain will move.

3. Your Beautiful Purpose; Live your Life for a Higher Reason. It's not just about positively impacting yourself, your employees, or your clients (although all this is amazing), but you can also impact your community, your environment, your world.

I am sure this sounds overwhelming, but remember what we are working on right now, my darling: baby steps. Set attainable goals. Leverage your team, talent, and resources. Realize that your impact is larger than you may realize already. Know that by helping one person, you may be setting an example to others to help one person, and this can quickly take on a movement of greater proportions.

4. Connect to Your Core Values like Your Heart Connects to Your Bloodlines. A great first step as a leader, as a person, as you, my angel, is to define your core values. What is important to you? Honesty? Integrity? Accountability? Perseverance? Advocacy? Make your own list of words that are meaningful to you. Make these words the pillars you lead your life by. Surround yourself with people who demonstrate similar values (and not just in what they say, but in what they do—the true measurement of character).

By following these values, you will find that you are in an 'upward spiral'. There's so much talk of 'downward spirals', whereas when one thing goes wrong, another follows, and so on. There should be more talk of the opposite—upward spirals—when good begets more good. It's a beautiful cycle and one that you should take pause in, appreciate, be grateful for, and then pass it forward.

5. Beyond Sight: Connect with Your Power of Visualization. This is particularly helpful during times of great importance. If you are fortunate to have the time and energy, consider your move before you make it. Let it play like a film inside your mind. More than just a dream, in these visualizations, replay the scene over and over again. Think of all possibilities and which action yields the best results. I try to consider who else will be impacted and how. Once I can see it, the best path forward, I then feel confident to live it.

And please know, my love, that in the act of living out these visual-izations, in the act of doing, yes, we will make mistakes. Just as you fall down now trying to waddle more than three steps, know that we are human and trying to achieve perfection is impossible and there-fore a waste of time and energy. Know too that you can learn so much in each little stumble. And the real measurement of character is often illustrated in the how and the why one gets back up and goes back at it.

Sometimes fear can paralyze us, leave us standing still, barely breathing. My sweet Ava, know this: life is about leaping. Faith is leaping into the unknown but knowing your light will guide you through regardless. Trust in your light. It's Godly. It's God.

6. You've Got This; Now Work It Out. You come from a long line of hard workers. Your great grandmother joined the Women's Army Corp in World War II, when your great grandfather joined the Navy, to end the global spread of extreme racism and dictatorial rule. Your father evacuated his entire company safely from the 33rd floor of a downtown NYC skyscraper on 9/11. Your mom birthed you, my greatest accomplishment, in a bathtub during the global pandemic. I wish we could give you a lifetime without human or natural disasters, but know this: when tested, your work ethic, perse-verance, faith, and courage will be there to overcome. You have fight in you, my little one. You have all of us, generations of strength and love, as your angels, cheering you on. You are never alone. But you must do the work.

Meaningful results come when you combine the following: hard work, strategy, planning, purposeful people, faith, and love. This world needs meaningful results. We need you, your talents, and your blessed work ethic.

Know that your hard, purposeful work will yield results. Never back down from work. Never fear work. It is a blessing, particularly for leaders like you, who can turn it into meaningful results. After all, not every farmer is blessed to yield a harvest. But for those who do, like you one day, consider how you can help feed those around you with your harvest. If you can, do. Connect with your community.

7. The Fundamental Human Need to Connect. I talk a lot about connection at work—the power of connecting networks. The power of communicating. This is a basic need for humanity. Think of cavemen and women drawing pictures of buffalo on walls with berry juice. In our earliest days, we as humans needed to share and storytell. I mention this as it's a great launching point for becoming a genuine leader. You may have heard the phrase 'leading blindly', but often I see leaders 'leading deafly', failing to listen. A connection is bilateral—a two-way street. Listen before you speak. Let your team and/or community know that you hear them. Try to use their word choice in your response back; speaking the same language is critical for better understanding. Connect with your heart, not just words.

8. Responsibility: Yes, Go Down With the Ship. Or ideally, try to make your ship stay afloat, please. But as a leader, the responsibility is yours. You are ultimately responsible for the well-being of your team, your family, your values. You will be held accountable for not just your actions but also the actions performed by the people you lead.

I talk a lot about creating 'an environment to succeed' at work. Does my team have the right tools, time, and collaboration with other talented colleagues to execute with true purpose and meaning? I literally ask myself this question every day, as it's my duty to ensure it.

When the day comes, and, my dear, I'm sure it will (as we are all human), and I am brought into the principal's office because of a rule you broke at school, I will hold myself accountable for not teaching you that rule. That is, until you break the same rule again, after you were taught it, and then I will hold you accountable.

Mind you, if it's a silly rule, we can work within our rights to amend it as well. Don't forget to question 'silliness', and by this I mean ignorance and biasness. Unfortunately, there's a lot of 'silliness' in this world. Question and rebel when needed. No good leaders blindly follow the rules. If it feels wrong to your core values, then question it. Again, be guided by the light inside you. If it feels inherently wrong, we can then build a plan to change it.

This, too, is your responsibility—to impact positive change in this world—so you can pass the world on to your children a little better than the one you inherited.

9. People Treat You as You Allow Them. Your father says this all the time to me, and at first, I rebelled against it. I thought of all the times when people are in the wrong place at the wrong time and bad things happen without their consent. This is sadly true but not what this statement refers to—it refers to what is in your control, and, my dear, you have a lot more control than you realize. Insist on being treated with respect. As such, people will naturally take your lead and treat you with respect accordingly.

And they should, as you are powerful. You are strong. When you walk into a conference room, go ahead and take the seat at the head of the table (assuming you've done the work necessary to earn it). But yes, always expect respect. You will receive it. The same is true in reverse, so expect great and positive things.

10. Fiercely Embrace Your Positivity. Positive thinking leads to positive visualizations leads to positive action leads to positive upward spirals. Life is too short for negative thinking. Try to limit or avoid wasting time and energy on negative thinking—this includes emotions like jealousy or hate.

The world needs more positive leadership to counterbalance all the darkness. When you find it difficult to find the silver lining in a situation, meditating on positivity helps. Simplicity helps. Prayer helps.

Take a moment and whisper your love and hopes to the great forces of positivity. Let your hair be caught again in the wind, as if you were going down that slide, and listen to the Lord's response in between the breeze.

Positivity is Godly. It's a strength that can comfort and heal and raise you.

And remember, too, that positivity is a choice, like balance and happiness. Your life, including your health and well-being, are better when you choose positivity. Embrace it—even fight for it when you must. It's worth it.

11. My Beautiful Sunflower, Plan for Your Growth, as I Promise, You Will Grow. Please never stand still, frozen in fear. Keep moving. Keep growing. If you want to be young forever, here's your answer: keep learning.

My stepfather used to say that education is the one thing that no one can ever take away from you, and it's mostly true. There are other things too—such as your faith, positivity, love, and happiness. No one can ever claim your essence—your light—that's yours and all yours. Embrace it. Grow it.

And remember, you can't grow if you don't plan for growth. Keep challenging yourself. If writing a book is your goal, albeit a rather large one, start by publishing a blog, then a series of blogs, and then write a chapter, and then a book. Yes, you can sit down one afternoon and bang out a book, but will it be the best you can do? Probably not. Maybe, but probably not. Always try your best. Either do it and do it well, or don't do it at all. And to do it well means having a plan for success.

Is the environment you are in conducive for success? Are you writing in the dark with a blunt pencil and a small scrap of paper? Or are you in an inspirational, lit room, with plenty of time before your deadline, typing away, with a clear outline and a fabulous cup of coffee?

I'm planning for growth right now with JSA. I am hiring for next year, as I still need to train and prepare the next generation of JSAers, for next year's additional clients, while keeping my current clients and team members engaged and growing.

You will find as you grow as a leader, so do the people you are leading. In fact, you are responsible for their growth, for their successes. My hope is that every person at my company becomes better and stronger, professionally and personally, by being part of JSA. And my hope is the same for my clients and the industry we collectively represent.

And, of course, my hope is for you. Ava, please know that as I write this, as you roll over in your crib a little restless, that I have all the hope and love in this world for you and your constant growth as you find your own way, listening to your own sweet light inside you.

12. The Two Limited Resources We Don't Discuss Enough: Your Time and Energy. You may find one day that your most valuable resources are your time and energy. This might cause you to giggle right now, as you are young and you have all the energy and time in the world, so much so that you crawl around in circles to try to burn it off. But when you can, save your time and energy for what's really important, not for unattainable goals. Live your life with joy and love and the desire to do good. Live each day knowing it could be your last but that you at least took full advantage of the short time on Earth that you were given.

Appreciate those who give you their energy and time, like your family, teachers, colleagues, and friends. Return their kindness and appreciate their devotion of their most precious resources to you and your vision.

Conversely, for those in your life who may be takers of your energy and time, try to limit their influence on you. Try to limit, if possible, the time you spend in their company. Instead, shower your attention and love on those who appreciate you, and, ideally, return their energy and love.

13. Lastly, Love. You were born from love. Love is already inside of you. Discover it. Cherish it. Share it. As one of your dad's favorite artists said, "The love you take is equal to the love you make." Show love in your leadership. Show love in your community.

By shining your light and energy, you are sharing your love outwardly, and it will return to you in spades. This is faith. This is true, meaningful impact. This is your legacy. As you are ours.

About the Author

JAYMIE SCOTTO CUTAIA

As one of the most influential women in marketing for the telecom and data center industries globally, Jaymie Scotto Cutaia founded Jaymie Scotto & Associates (JSA), an award-winning, industry-focused public relations, marketing, and event planning firm, over sixteen years ago. Throughout this time, JSA has represented hundreds of brands in thousands of meaningful campaigns and headlines, impacting change and connectivity.

For example, in 2010, when Haiti was struck by a massive earthquake, JSA created the Telecom Relief Fund and rallied the industry to provide support and funding for those in need. Recently, JSA created the Women Speaking Initiative (WSI) to collect and distribute speaking profiles of outstanding women in our industry, to encourage a more equitable representation of women on the speaking circuit.

In the *X-Factor: The Spiritual Secrets Behind Successful Executives & Entrepreneurs,* Jaymie dedicates her chapter to her one-year-old daughter, Ava. The chapter is a letter to Ava, to offer guidance, support and best practices that have served Jaymie best over the years, while leading JSA with faith, heart and purpose.

In addition to Ava and JSA, Jaymie cites her husband, Rory, and their marriage and courtship of over seventeen years, as one of her top blessings.

Website: www.jsa.net
LinkedIn: https://www.linkedin.com/in/jaymiescotto/

FOUR

Mathias Fritzen

YOU ARE SO MUCH MORE: HOW THE DEEPEST
UNDERSTANDING OF WHO WE ARE–OUR CORE
IDENTITY–SHAPES OUR REALITY AND DETERMINES THE
COURSE OF OUR LIVES

It may appear to you that the stories you're about to read are both incoherent and highly personal and that they have nothing to do with you and your life. I invite you—for the sake of curious exploration—to consider that the opposite is true. What if the underlying message of my stories bears the same transformational power for you? Close your eyes for a minute and put aside everything you know. As my teacher likes to say: *You can pick it up later. It won't go anywhere.*

Now that your cup is empty, I invite you to follow me on a journey about personal development and spiritual awakening. Read with your heart rather than your mind. Discard what doesn't touch you and take in deeply that which resonates. When I get the chance to meet you, dear reader, I will do the same while listening to your stories. Maybe they will take my life to the next level.

First We'll Try to Save Your Arm

Do you know Parkour? Exactly, that's the sport where people jump from rooftop to rooftop. In the early 2000s, I happened to be part of a crazy bunch pioneering the sport in Germany. A few weeks before

I had the chance to perform at a series of shows for a big car company, I was at the peak of my physical abilities. More than a decade of martial arts training made me feel invincible, and now, on top of that, I was living and breathing Parkour. Seeing through the eyes of a Parkour athlete, every city becomes a playground. Can you imagine how it feels to swing from one tree to another without anyone even noticing that you're up there? Powerful.

So here we were—my good friend Deniz, a few rookies, and me. After some training and exploring around, we found ourselves standing in front of a giant tree that was spreading its branches wide over the surrounding walls. There it was: my next challenge. Running up from the top of a wall, I took a big leap toward the tree. Midair I reached for one of the branches. Got it! But it was slippery. And me…too fast! The branch slipped out of my hands, and I found myself falling, headfirst. Somehow I managed to brace myself with my left arm. I sprung back to my feet, swearing because I had failed. Then I saw it. My arm….

Now everything happens in super slow-motion. The rookies are running away. Someone is shouting from a window: *Who's gonna clean up all that blood?* I patch up my arm with a sweatshirt. Deniz arrives with screeching tires. I'm thinking: *Don't drip on the fancy leather!* Somehow nothing hurts, but I'm sweating like crazy. I'm on a stretcher in the elevator headed to the emergency room. A crowd of white coats surround me. There's only one question in my head. I hear myself asking: *When can I get back to training?* One of the doctors answers coolly: *First, we'll try to save your arm.*

They did. But that's not the only magic that took place. The accident happened only five minutes away from a clinic specialized in vascular surgery, with the best physicians directly on site. My ambulance coach was Deniz's father's five hundred-horsepower sedan. I can't recall us having ever used this particular car before or after that day. I lost half of my blood but didn't need a blood transfusion. I had a bad infection in my elbow and it fully healed. My girlfriend's car took her to the hospital almost every day and broke down right after I left the hospital—five weeks later. I met the absolute best physiotherapist and osteopath: a bulky dude with Russian roots who was so damn sensitive that he could feel a single hair under seven layers of paper. What a blessing!

One year later, I went back to see the head physician and show him the results. I guess it was more common to sue a doctor those days than to share a success story. He didn't recognize me at first but, man, did he recognize my arm. He was blown away by what he saw. He moved my arm around in all directions like a little boy who had just gotten a new toy crane for Christmas.

I am incredibly grateful. At this moment, I am writing to you using that exact arm. It's no longer my arm alone. It's nothing less than a co-creative masterpiece.

For such a long time I had thought that I was a Parkour athlete. The training, the philosophy, the way of life—it was indistinguishably intertwined with me—it had become me. Unthinkable what would happen if that was taken away from me. Who would I be without it? No one.

What I was searching for in Parkour had finally found me: freedom. Not the freedom to do fancy moves. A freedom from something. A freedom from identity. Mathias the Parkour pioneer went bust. I still love him and wear his clothes from time to time. But I know now that I'm not him.

What If That Nutcase Is Right?

After about ten minutes of listening to the audiobook *The Power of Now*, I couldn't take it anymore. The narrator's voice (Eckhart Tolle himself) was annoying me so much that I had to turn it off. Esoteric nonsense!

Years later, the printed version fell into my hands, randomly, of course. But was it really a coincidence? I decided to give it another try, and yet again, I couldn't do it. *He's circling around the same thing over and over again*, I thought. *By all means, this is not a good book!*

For some reason, the annoying, small, yellow book kept reappearing in my life. But it wasn't until I hit rock bottom going through separation with my wife that I picked up the book again. Only then, sitting on the floor of my thirty square meter apartment with mold on the walls, did it hit me like a brick: *What if this is not just a book? What if it's actually true? What if that nutcase is right?*

That's when I went haywire. Like a crazy professor, I turned my apartment into a lab. I scanned every page for its core teachings and extracted them onto Post-it Notes. Little yellow squares soon covered my bedroom door, the kitchen cabinets, and my bathroom mirror.

Every morning I read through them before leaving for work. In my regular job I worked on autopilot. Most of my attention was fixated on observing what was going on inside of me—always trying to match up my observations with Tolle's teachings. I put *The Power of Now* to the hardest tests I could imagine, and what can I say? It passed.

There has always been, and there will always be just here and now. For most of my life up to that point, I'd been escaping the present moment living in a world of thoughts—past and future. Wow.

Just a few weeks prior to this realization, I thought I was getting pretty close to having a coherent idea about myself and life in general. You could have put me in any discussion, and I would've had a thought-out line of arguments prepared for all kinds of topics, or so I thought.

The Mathias knows-it-all identity crumbled under *The Power of Now*, and I got relegated back to basecamp. There I was, having to admit that I don't know much of anything at all. But, man, was I onto something! I could feel that very clearly.

If God Is Everywhere, Why Is He Not Here?

I was born into a Christian family. We went to church on Wednesday evenings and twice on Sundays. Looking back, I felt sheltered and cared for in this community. There were a few priests that I liked in particular. Sometimes they did house visits and we talked and prayed together. I enjoyed the energy and presence that I felt in those moments.

Service was a strange mix of meditation and boredom for me. I always had a hard time listening to the words. It was more the energy that got me. After I heard a story about someone in our community who allegedly had the ability to see angels, I looked to the altar, actively blurring my vision and trying to see them too. It didn't work.

I did what I was told. I believed. But I was also a curious child with many questions. Nobody seemed to have the answers, and I was also told-off. *Stop asking!* Who was this omnipotent, all-powerful God, that cannot handle the questions of a ten-year-old child?

Looking around I saw many gentle and warmhearted souls. But I also witnessed them dwelling in victimhood and holding on to the idea of salvation in the afterlife. *What about this life? If God was everywhere, He has to be here, too!* I couldn't sit around on the church pew any longer. I had to find Him…or Her.

In that moment the devout believer made way for the rebellious seeker in me. You see, identity collapsing doesn't mean that it's all gone. Quite the contrary—identity has the tendency to reassemble itself or shift its shape.

Intoxicated Insight

One of my best friends and I grew up garden-to-garden to each other. Saying hi was as easy as a walk through the backyard. We spent so much time together as kids, and today he was getting married. I was happy for him and his wife, but it also felt surreal since I was just about to get divorced. What a strange course of events.

We all shared a big circle of mutual friends at that time. Many of them were there that day. My wife decided not to come. There I was, in my friend's parents' backyard getting drunk. Emotional turmoil on the inside, childhood memories on the outside, a lot of happy people around me, and a fake smile on my face. I felt misplaced. This wasn't my reality anymore.

I had planned to sleep at my parents' place that night. It had gotten late and I didn't want to wake them up, so I decided to take the long way around the block. By that time, I was quite drunk and it felt like it was taking forever.

It was in this unlikely moment when, out of nowhere, a thought entered my mind: *If the teachings are right and I'm not my body, then I'm not really drunk either…*and WHAM! In an instant I find myself in a bird's-eye view looking down on my drunk body stumbling forward. The experience of being drunk had vanished. With a crystal clear consciousness, I was observing my body walking home.

Wow, that's weird. Is intoxicated insight even spiritually correct? Am I making this up? A few thoughts like that were bubbling up and passing by. I couldn't follow them. I was too mesmerized by this amazing experience. Wait…I? My body was down there and I was up here. Who was having this experience?

When I woke up the next day I wasn't hovering over my body anymore. I was definitely in my body. My throbbing head testified to it. However, I knew beyond a doubt that I was not my body (and that I should be drinking less alcohol in the future).

My First Term of Employment: As Short as This Paragraph

After twelve years of school and another six years studying commu-nications-design, I got my first job: junior art director in one of my favorite advertising agencies. Man, was I excited for this job! One day in that first week at work after finishing all my tasks, I packed my bag at 6:00 p.m. I was ready to leave when my superior said: *Are you working only half-days? You are not really excited for this job, are you?* Was this a joke? Whatever it was, something about it felt really wrong to me. My stomach turned upside down. Deep inside I knew right then and there that this wasn't for me. It took me six more months to muster up enough courage to quit. The foundation stone for my self-employment was laid—many fantastic years together with bril-liant people that were all, in fact, working half-days.

I Don't Need a Shrink!

I'm fine, thank you for asking. I will figure this out myself! I don't need a shrink. (Me before my first therapy session.)

You have to listen! You won't believe the mind-blowing insight I just had! (Me on the phone with my parents after every single therapy session.)

I want more! Where's the next Zen monastery? Where can I get my coach certifi-cation? (Me after my last therapy session.)

The Serum Is Already In

From my perspective, personal development and spiritual awak-ening are both segments of the same journey. Up to a certain point in life, our persona (egoic identity) is being created in a rather unconscious process. We gather impressions from our parents, friends, colleagues, and the world around us. We model our mentors and impersonate that which provides us with the most attention and love in return.

When this process shifts from an unconscious to a conscious one, we call it personal development. We are now involved in actively shaping our persona according to our own visions and dreams. Many empowerment teachings promote the principle that *we are the creators of our own worlds.*

Personal development eventually culminates into spiritual awakening. We've achieved everything that we set out to achieve. We ticked all the boxes and cannot find another answer to the question of *what's next?* That's when our attention turns inward.

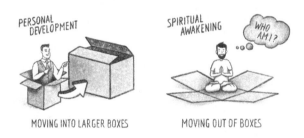

MOVING INTO LARGER BOXES   MOVING OUT OF BOXES

Why am I doing all this, and where does it lead me? What is this life really about? Who am I on the deepest level? These are some of the questions that can come up. Experiencing the answers is spiritual awakening. It might sound cryptic, but it's really not just about mental understanding. It's about directly and intimately experiencing the answer —being the answer.

Wherever you are on your journey, it's very likely that you encounter life-changing, transformative, or otherwise defining moments every once in a while. From the outside they might seem small, but in your own experience, they make a world of difference.

This was one of these moments for me:

I'm on a retreat, taking contemplative walks around the resort a few times each day. One round trip takes about forty-five minutes. Passing by the edge of the forest, I'm on a dusty path lined by beautiful cork trees. I'm reflecting on a few teachings that stuck with me from the morning. One in particular keeps repeating itself over and over again in my mind: *The serum is already in.*

The serum must be some kind of high potency concoction, I thought. *Once I drink it, it does its job automatically. I'm not sure when it will take full effect, but it's certain that it will since it's already in. I already drank it. Wait...I already drank it? I did. And there's nothing that I could possibly do to stop it from taking effect? There's nothing I could do. It will take effect.* I knew that to be true with every single cell in my body.

I picture how *the serum* went into my belly to eventually explode there like a bomb. It's just a matter of time. It's inevitable.

Of course, I didn't drink any actual serum. It was a metaphor for focusing my attention on spiritual awakening and taking in the teachings like I would do with a serum.

If there's a strong desire and urgency in our hearts, when we focus all our attention on this one goal, then the serum is already in. *What is your heart calling for?*

One Thousand Hours with Bob-Marley-Santa-Claus

At some point it became apparent to me that I needed a spiritual teacher. One that I could trust, like Bob-Marley-Santa-Claus. Bob-Marley-Santa-Claus? That's how I jokingly described my teacher Mooji's outer appearances to my friends.

Trusting someone with my life, or at least with my sanity, would take some time. In my case it took nine months and more than one thousand hours of Mooji videos before I actually dared to participate in one of his retreats.

There I was. Sitting and meditating. Ready to fully let go. Instantly, everything that I had felt before reaching *the inner door* came back—the sweat, the rapid heartbeat, the terror.

Everything that you can perceive is not you. I am not my body. I am not my mind. I am not my fear. Excruciating pain washed over me. This was it. I was certain that I was about to die right then and there—in the midst of all of these people, in a tent somewhere in Portugal. *So be it*, I thought.

Sizzling hot lava was flowing through my body and out of my arms and hands. It felt like something was burning and melting away. I use this metaphor for lack of better words to describe the indescribable.

I don't know how much time passed…but at some point the pain was over. There was just a deep silence within me that slowly but steadily filled up with unconditional love. I was neither dead nor mad. There was just a pure love that I'd never felt before.

You have to understand that I grew up in Duisburg, Germany. Not so long ago, the city was still coughing up steel, fire, and hard work. Its people are straightforward and outspoken. It was *the Duisburger* in me that scanned the crowd for the ugliest man I could find. It didn't change a thing. I loved him just as much. It was absolutely overwhelming.

It's so Simple

I was in the tent again. Days were merging in a mesmerizing blur. The same sentence that had been so soothing before now turned against me: *Everything that you can perceive is not you.*

Even unconditional love was perceivable and therefore…wasn't me. In a split second »I« exploded. I couldn't find my person, ego, identity—you name it. Gone! What felt like absolute freedom came with big laughter. *Where was I?* Everywhere. The separation between me and everything around me had vanished. There was just…*this*. And *this* wasn't anything foreign after all. It had been here all along, hidden in plain sight. Home.

What Jesus taught in John 14:6 made perfect sense to me now: *I am the way, and the truth, and the life. No one comes to the Father except through me. If you had known Me, you would know My Father as well.*

It is the »I« that needs to be known—the »I« as in *Identity.* It's equally simple as it is easy to overlook. *Who is this Me? Who is this I, deep within you?*

Conclusion

We can think of our identity as the box that we're living in. As much as it enables us to do certain things, it also limits us. At first we fall in love with its enabling qualities. Then, as we mature into a particular identity, we become more and more aware of an inner impulse to expand and outgrow it. Eventually, we move houses: from a small identity-box, we move into a bigger (or different) one until we finally decide to move out of the boxes altogether.

Each time we go through a transformation like this, our identity is expanding. The more it expands, the more inclusive it becomes. With increasing inclusiveness of our identity, we develop as servant leaders—effortlessly.

Isn't it most natural to care for what you experience as part of yourself? Think of a tree as your extended lungs. Sadhguru explains it well: *What you exhale, the tree inhales. What the tree exhales, you inhale.* The tree is a vital part of you, and so is the entire cosmos, including your most annoying colleague at work. They are just as alive as you are. Alive—a life. Different expressions, but essentially one life.

If you take a closer look at all of the little stories that I've shared with you, you find that they have three underlying principles in common. These principles are vital ingredients to transformation. They became the foundational pillars of my work.

1. Fresh Perspectives: The key to create change is to do things differently, think differently, and ultimately look at life from a different perspective.
2. Self-Responsibility: *It's all in our hands.* Is that good news or bad news? It's our choice! Taking full self-responsibility is the end of victimhood.
3. Direct Experience: This is not theory. This is practice. Everything flows from head to heart to hand, directly applicable in our everyday lives.

These principles provide a solid outline for orientation. True power, however, lies somewhere else. Deep transformation happens beyond concepts. It's about presence. It's about being present with someone. I mean truly being with someone—full-on awareness. Nothing remains unseen in this light.

My slightly unconventional path might be the most comforting *spiritual secret* that I can share with you. It's not a blueprint. Quite the contrary: It illustrates that there is no *correct* path. Instead, there are many, and yours is one of them. The only question is: *Are you truly owning it, here and now?*

About the Author

MATHIAS FRITZEN

Mathias is all-in for truth without detours—straightforward and integrated. He has been called the master of clarity.

In his chapter he reveals why the deepest understanding of who we are—our core identity—shapes our reality and determines the course of our lives.

As an award-winning digital creative, Mathias knows how to turn complexity into clarity (clients like Lufthansa, Telekom, DHL, etc.). Pioneering the extreme sport Parkour made him an expert in overcoming obstacles (shows for Adidas, RTL, ZDF, etc.). Having played more than two million hands of poker, he knows exactly how to read people. After a life-changing experience in meditation, he discovered that all of the above is play.

Mathias now coaches the key players of tomorrow's conscious and integrated society (certification: ICF PCC, NLP-MP, TRuST HC, etc.).

Visit Mathias' website: MathiasFritzen.com
Watch his free Clarity Clips:
MathiasFritzen.com/clarity-clips

FIVE

Angela E. Kochuba

THE PLATINUM JOURNEY

This chapter is dedicated to my children, parents of children with special needs, and all the early intervention healthcare professionals, who are saints in my life's story.

Sunset Beach, North Carolina, USA (2017)

As I packed a sling bag with water and sunscreen, I announced to my family I was finally going to hike to the famous Kindred Spirit Mailbox. The mailbox drew attention in 2017 when it landed Sunset Beach fourth on National Geographic's list of the 21 Best Beaches in the World. Many have said visiting the mailbox is a spiritual experience regardless of their religion. It's a cherished community mailbox full of tattered and well-loved journals. The mailbox whispers an invitation, and visitors who hear the calling open a journal and pen their hopes, dreams, fears, struggles, grief, and prayers. Once the journals are full, they are replaced with new ones as if signaling to all visitors the opportunity to refresh and renew.

To my surprise, my three teens wanted to join me on the hike. My husband dropped us off at the last beach access point, and we strolled along the wooden walkway perched above the grassy dunes and wildlife boasting deer, foxes, rabbits, and random wild goats. Entering onto the beach, we left behind our flip flops and walked into the serene picture of a wide strand of beach and a seemingly endless sky of vibrant watercolors.

Directional Sign to Kindred Spirit Mailbox

Only three miles long, Sunset Beach is the southernmost barrier island of North Carolina, and throughout the years, as sand was magically added to the island, it connected with the Bird Island Coastal Reserve. Once considered a nude bather's secret location, the reserve now boasts a family environment where people walk their dogs and hunt for sand dollars in the long stretches of gentle water and silky sand.

Strolling along the edges of the waves, we collected shells and chatted about our lives. As a mother of teens, I love to observe and listen to how they interact with one another, and, thankfully, the beach brings out the best in them every time. These are the moments when my working mother's guilt fades into the background.

Therapy Rooms in the Washington, DC Area (2004)

As a rambunctious one year old, our joyful son would run around the house yelling to his seven-year-old brother, "Joey, chase me!" Alarmingly, we watched our youngest son quickly lose all speech along with his ability to smile and kiss us. A dear friend mentioned my son's sudden decline to a rather famous autism expert in the area. Even though he had a current waiting list of four years, he told my friend he would squeeze us into his overflowing schedule. Dr. Greenspan enthusiastically stated, "I'm going to save the emotional and social life of that child." He had been frustrated with the lack of support for early intervention and was seeing children much older than our one-year-old son.

When my husband, child, and I walked into Dr. Greenspan's home office, we were indeed interrupting Dr. Greenspan's lunch, which I distinctly recall included a juicy pear our son wanted to share. By the end of the appointment, our son was diagnosed with dyspraxia, not autism, and Dr. Greenspan said, "We'll get him cooking!" He shared his referrals for additional assessments and therapists along with our first homework assignment. It was the first time I'd ever heard of Floortime, and as the website states, I was to engage with our son at "his level—both developmentally and physically—in order to maximize communicating, interacting, and learning. This means getting on the floor to engage the child's attention." I was to conduct eight sessions a day for twenty minutes per session. This wasn't a one-hour-per-week therapy situation. With a developmental physician's prescription for daily professional therapy along with this nearly three-hour daily Floortime assignment, it meant goodbye to my full-time career, which I loved.

As a mom, my children counted on me at home and at school, and I even morphed myself into a dyspraxia researcher in the wee hours of the night. As a wife who wanted to cry and collapse onto her husband's shoulder, my husband needed me to stay mentally tough when a Major General explained lives would literally be lost without my husband's efforts traveling with and supporting the military in war zones. I don't need to go into the details about maintaining decades-long friendships and efforts to keep a pinky toe in the working world, but believe me when I tell you it was one of the toughest times in my life. I would often feel like I wasn't "enough." I bet you a cup of hand-crafted coffee I'm not the only person who's ever felt stretched thin and inadequate.

I'd usually join my son in his therapy sessions to ensure I asked for and understood homework assignments. On days when my exhaustion was overwhelming, I'd sit in the waiting room fighting back silent tears that would eventually waterfall. I'd sit in my own version of Pity Town knowing I'd have to pull myself together in less than fifty minutes to transform back into the relentless superhero version of myself.

Frightened and hopeful parents in those therapy waiting rooms formed their own support networks. I figured I couldn't control what was happening to my family, but maybe, by reaching out and being vulnerable and willing to share experiences and information, I could help someone else who was fighting back tears. We turned our personal sorrows into helping one another. I'm grateful for their stories that wove into mine, holding me up like steel rods.

For the next several years, I crawled through homemade ball pits and sifted for toy animals in the sensory rice bin I created from a plastic underbed storage container and a fifty-pound bag of rice. Although I feared my brain power was being dulled with "ba, pa, ma" speech exercises, my child taught me one of the most valuable leadership lessons that has served me well throughout my career: *leadership isn't about the leader.*

While battling insurance companies that consistently refused to acknowledge physician prescriptions, searching for the best therapists, discussing goals with physicians, and even fighting through unsettling comments from extended family members, I sharply realized leadership is often about advocating for your people and giving them the tools and experiences they need to grow and thrive. It's often not about my brain power; it's about growing and inspiring the brain power of others through a willingness to believe in them and never give up on meeting their needs.

When the "if you want it done right, do it yourself" adage could no longer work for me, I dragged my fiercely independent mind into realizing I can't always be the one to do the job. I learned I didn't always have the answers, and I felt vulnerable and raw until I realized I could cultivate relationships and count on others. My child and his speech, occupational, and physical therapists shaped a new and powerful phrase by their actions: if you want it done right, pour your efforts into others who will succeed for you. I learned how important it is to acknowledge, honor, combine, and collaborate with differing skillsets.

In the Gospel of Matthew, Jesus says, "Do unto others as you would have them do unto you." As a Christian, I learned this ethical principle early in life and learned many people, regardless of religion, believe in this statement as a way of life. It's known as the Golden Rule, which is to treat others the way you want to be treated. While struggling with the fear my son may never speak again, my prayers started each day before my feet hit the floor and ended my nights as I drifted to sleep. I soon realized God put me on a path to learn that people are often not where you expect them to be in life, and you don't always know everything about everyone. Yes, you can treat them the way you'd want to be treated, but I also realized it's important to meet people where they are and not where we expect them to be. I learned the value of the Golden Rule used with the Platinum Rule, which is to do unto others as they would want to be done to them. Or, better yet, do unto others according to their needs and not our own desires.

When I finally let go of expectations found on childhood development charts indicating how many words my child should have by age two, I could focus on what his unique developmental needs were as an individual. The more progress he'd make, the less heartache and disappointment I'd feel. I was then able to pour myself into my son and provide every support I could with his needs as the priority. Many parents think children should adapt to them or respect them simply because they are the parents, yet when we're willing to bend and literally get down on another person's level to see the world the way they do, we can better provide what they need to thrive. This was the phase in my life when I had to let go of the control freak in me, practice patience, learn imperfection has value, and realize I didn't always have to be the hero; I could support and prepare others to lead and become their own heroes.

After several years, when my child was thriving and released from daily occupational, physical, and speech therapies, I was able to focus more on my career again. Knocked down to the literal floor, I eventually learned that being in a support role to help others develop is a gift.

Sunset Beach, North Carolina, USA (2017)

After years of grit, I was excelling as an independent contractor, who ranked at the top of consultants and speakers in a large consulting and training company. My small, woman- and minority-owned business was growing, and as a team, we were thriving. Finally, I carved out time to take my long-awaited trip to the Kindred Spirit. Walking along the shoreline where the sand dollars dotted the watery edges of waves, I unknowingly carried a heavy emotional boulder along with years of guilt for never being "enough." This isn't rare; many people lead a life of giving. We give of ourselves to our families, colleagues, friends, and businesses without replenishing.

As I walked alongside my now three teens, I seemed carefree… thought I was carefree. Then, I opened the famous Kindred Spirit Mailbox perched high among the dunes.

Kindred Spirit Mailbox

When I read the stories left behind by others, I wept. Reading the entries is akin to revealing autobiographies that morph into the self-help section in a library. Those stories transformed me. Once again, I was reminded of the lesson my child taught me years ago: meet people where they are and not where we expect or want them to be. I was reconnected with the reminder that everyone is going through trials, and we all want to contribute to the world. This transformed my approach to relationships and life. Leaders, with the right mindset, can allow others to flourish rather than shame in judgment. We can support one another and help carry our respective boulders; we don't have to be alone. True wealth is in the relationships we build and how we inspire others to be the best version of themselves. Through this mindset we purposefully choose each day, we build commitment rather than resistance or mere compliance.

As I prepared to write my Kindred Spirit journal entry that I didn't know I'd want to share, I sat on the nearby wooden bench and prayed; I continued to weep as I wrote my thankful entry to God. As the ink flowed and I gazed at the cotton candy sunset, I felt my boulder roll away into the ocean, swept away by the gentle waves. It was as if I had hit the reset button and pure gratefulness remained. Until that moment, I hadn't felt the full release of my boulder that had grown for more than fourteen years.

My teens were confused about my tears, but my oldest son wisely let me sit on the wooden bench and gaze at the sunset without a spoken word. He led his younger siblings on a walk past the mailbox toward the North Carolina and South Carolina state line marked by a rocky jetty.

When they returned, I was able to meet them on the walk back toward the beach cottage. Grounded in faith, I often joke about how many times God has to hit me in the head with a brick before I catch on that everything He does is *always* in my best interests. So, that day, I let all my anxieties fade into the sunset.

"Intimacy in the Dunes", Copyright © A.J. Kochuba, Art Gallery AJKochuba.com

Please allow me to provide hope; I'm happy and proud to say that our son is attending a top 10 university pursuing science and visual art. Getting down on his level allowed him to thrive. I often say dyspraxia was a blessing in disguise for our son. It gave him a strong drive to communicate, an incredible attention span built in daily therapy sessions, perseverance, and the courage to ignite his creativity and explore. Finding the gifts in each person and nurturing a sense of belonging and acceptance for who they are, rather than who we want them to be, allows each person to develop their strengths and shine.

I'm also happy to add you can take a hiatus from your career to care for a loved one, whether a child, aging parent, or yourself. It's possible to find what you love to do and succeed.

In my profession, I'm reminded of the strength that can emerge from bending. When we meet people where they are rather than where we expect them to be, and when we are willing to see more than one way forward—understanding our way is not the only "right" way to success—I believe our self-reflection reaps benefits. When we stop dictating and put our inner selves aside, we can practice the Platinum Rule and coach individuals into finding the right path for them, which ultimately benefits the team and organization. As a parent, I'm determined to support my children and their dreams, and it's the same mentality in the workplace. When supervisors take on their employees' dreams as their own and find ways to make those dreams come to life, the result is commitment and loyalty—results that ring throughout an organization.

I'm more in tune to my intellectual, emotional, physical, and spiritual growth than I was years ago. I hope I'm a better person than who I was back then, and I'm grateful for how God is sculpting me. If you aren't Christian, you can still apply these same lessons. To connect to your spirituality is to access your deepest core values and be aligned with your true sense of purpose. Have I figured it all out yet? No! But, now I know I should take the time to balance all four factors—intellectual, emotional, physical, and spiritual—to gain strength. I hope never to devalue the importance of mindfulness. For me, I can't attain true mindfulness without God, but however you engage in your spiritual journey, may it be fruitful and provide the overwhelming benefits I've found.

Shell Tree Located at 40th Street Beach Access
Walkway

At the Kindred Spirit Mailbox, we are connected by our humanity regardless of religion, race, country of origin, socioeconomic background, gender, or age. People of all faiths go to unburden themselves, to connect with their spirituality and nature. Read the powerful stories and step into another person's flip flops. Take time to let go of your boulders and refresh, and before you leave, find a sand dollar or shell to leave on the special memory tree on the 40th St walkway. You can leave a little mark saying you were here to connect with the world, ready to let go of the old and step onto the street pavement of your rejuvenated "platinum journey."

⊏══⊐

15 Self-Reflection Questions for Platinum-Minded Leaders to Consider

1. Do I practice the Golden Rule, treating others *as I want to be treated*?

2. Do I practice the Platinum Rule, treating others *as they want to be treated*?

3. Am I daring enough to lead others differently? Although I can influence others, I cannot control how others lead, but *I can control how I choose to lead*. Am I willing to take a risk and lead with the Platinum Rule (even if no other leaders around me are)?

4. Am I stoic in my leadership style, or do I adapt to the needs of others? Am I meeting people where they are? Am I giving people what they need, not only what I think they should need?

5. Do I advocate for others? Do I genuinely care about others and invest in their successes?

6. Do I free myself from thinking, *if I want it done right, I should do it myself*? Do I think there is only one "right way," which is my way, to accomplish a task or solve a problem? Am I open-minded to others and their viewpoints?

7. Am I shutting others down with disapproving looks and negative comments? Am I walking into meetings knowing all the answers, or am I truly listening to what others contribute?

8. Do I believe in and embrace diversity? Do I accept others and include them? Do I ensure my colleagues feel a sense of belonging in the workplace? Do I find each person's strengths and treasure each person's individuality?

9. Am I finding time to connect with and help others develop? Do I believe only one hour of time can make a significantly positive impact? (Think about how Dr. Greenspan was willing to squeeze in

an extra hour of time to positively change the course of a child's life. Although we never saw Dr. Greenspan again, he made a difference in only one hour.)

10. Am I patient?

11. Am I kind to myself? It's easy to get caught up in expectations.

12. Do I balance myself intellectually, emotionally, physically, and spiritually? Is there an area I could improve?

13. Do I take time to practice mindfulness? Do I take time to be fully present, aware, and focused?

14. Am I resilient? Can I embrace pressure, stay diligent, and build mental toughness for myself and my colleagues?

15. What is my spiritual secret, my X-factor?

About the Author

ANGELA E. KOCHUBA

Angela E. Kochuba lives with her husband, three children, and four dogs in North Carolina. They split their time between the Research Triangle Park area and the shore.

Angela has been a service-oriented entrepreneur since she was fifteen years old when she co-founded a successful training corporation. Her entrepreneurial spirit was enriched by earning her BS at the McIntire School of Commerce and her MBA at the Darden School of Business at the University of Virginia.

She is the founder and managing director of Federal Training Academy and is fully engaged in the success of its clients. She is a leadership expert with more than twenty years of experience working directly with every department in the US Federal Government and other global clients. She is a dynamic, global speaker and change management consultant who is committed to positive, job-related results linking people and missions in an agile world.

When she isn't working, you can find her cheering on the sidelines of her children's events, walking barefoot on the beach as a mindful mermaid, playing tennis or pickleball, or reading while wrapped in a blanket with one of her dogs in her lap and a cup of coffee by her side.

As a foodie, who is Amerasian with family dating back to the American Revolution, her favorite meals are when multiple generations of family and friends are gathered in conversation dining on Asian cuisine.

Join Angela's learning community on her website: FederalTraining-Academy.com
LinkedIn: https://www.linkedin.com/in/angela-kochuba/
Twitter: @AngelaKochuba

SIX

Rishi Kumar

WHAT HAPPENS WHEN LEADERSHIP IS PEPPERED WITH SPIRITUALITY?

The true leader is concerned primarily with the welfare of others, not with his own comfort or prestige.

—J. Oswald Sanders

My name is Rishi Kumar, and I am an IT executive transformation leader and advisor to large enterprises. Interestingly, my name also represents my spiritual side, as Rishi in Hindi also denotes saints and scientists.

We live in a world that cares about economic growth. Living to fulfill aspirations, to collect a paycheck, and to secure a pension, we spend hours a month going to the office and working without reflecting on the meaning behind the work. But it is essential to watch our environment and work with our spirit to inspire others and reach our personal goals. My aspirations led me to open two start-ups (now closed) and to work with different organizations like Xansa (now knowns as Sopra Steria), Computer Science Corporation (now known as DXC Technologies), Tata Consultancy Services, Cognizant Technology Solutions, Virtusa Corporation, and CGI Inc. I am currently working for Pactera EDGE.

I have also been giving back to society since my school days. I loved helping orphans, teaching in government schools, conducting health checkups, participating in various campaigns like the Yamuna cleaning campaign, and doing many other activities with CSR associations and NGOs. More recently, I have focused on: helping youth with career guidance; mentorship; helping start-ups; and supporting initiatives focused on community building. I received accolades and recognition for my efforts and was recently awarded with the Man of Excellence Award 2021 from the Indian Achievers Forum for outstanding professional achievements and contribution to nation-building.

Is Spiritual Leadership the Answer to All Modern-Day Work Problems?

Since COVID-19 affected the entire world and companies are focusing more on digitization and digital transformation with a work-from-anywhere style, leadership principles are focused more on servant leadership. Servant leadership's important characteristics are: listening, empathy, healing, awareness, conceptualization, foresight, persuasion, conceptualization, foresight, stewardship, growth for people, and building community. In my experience, there are many similarities between those characteristics and the characteristics of a spiritual awakening. When I was leading a team of more than two hundred people and managing a large client portfolio, ensuring everyone's motivation and growth were part of my key responsibilities. Being empathetic and a good listener always helped me cover this part. You cannot understand another person until you have some kind of self-awareness, and that is only possible when you are being spiritual.

Spirituality affects all aspects of one's life. People look up to a leader who can create something that other people could not think of at the workplace. A good leader can foresee that which others cannot. Spiritual elements make these things possible. One needs to experience life beyond a body and intellect to create a new possibility.

Mastery over yourself and your inner nature will help free you from outside limitations.

What Is the Driving Force Here?

From my own experience, faith has been a driving force. There is nothing possible without faith. Indian culture is steeped in spirituality and daily practices for inner wellbeing. My mother has been the greatest influencer in my life, and my father has been my greatest strength. I grew up seeing my mother following her daily rituals and oozing positivity all the time. Spirituality has been rooted since childhood. We learned that God is Omnipotent, Omniscience, and Omnipresent. We believe in this based on our faith.

I have experienced innumerable incidents in life where I felt the presence and protection of a higher form. One incident where I felt God's presence was when I got married and went to court for my marriage certificate in Kanpur with my wife in a hired auto. We got out of the auto, and after about ten minutes, we noticed we were missing something—our file containing all critical documents, including educational degrees and passports. The file had all the proof of my US job and journey. There was no way I could go back to the United States. All my dreams came crashing down like a pack of cards.

I think Kanpur was the worst place to lose the files. I told my friends and family what happened, but what could we do? Where could we find that auto? Will the auto driver understand the importance of the documents? I gave up hope. But my father did not. He roamed the city without any real direction looking for the driver and inquiring from the occasional passers-by. I was not a fan of this approach because there were probably more than a hundred auto drivers in the city, and the chances of finding the right one were almost equivalent to finding a pin in a desert. We were all feeling defeated and discouraged, except my father.

After a frantic search for a few hours, my father returned with the file that carried the documents. I was gasping in amazement and looked up to the universe with my heart full of gratitude. However, a voice from somewhere told me that at that moment, my father was my God. This incident made me understand that God is everywhere. It drove home the point that God appears in front of us in different forms, at different places, and even reassures us using a different voice every single day. After this we flew to the United States, lived in many different states, learned about different cultures, made new friends, and gained a lot of experience professionally and personally.

No other land has seen as much work toward human consciousness as Indian culture has. I am reminded of Mark Twain, one of the greatest intellectuals of the previous century. He came to India and had a good guide who took him to the right places. When he was leaving, he said, "So far as I am able to judge, nothing has been left undone, either by man or nature, to make India the most extraordinary country that the sun visits on his rounds. Nothing seems to have been forgotten, nothing overlooked."

Indian cultural contexts, mythologies, scriptures, and philosophies link up with our way of working. Steve Correa, in his book "The Indian Boss at Work", asserts: ""There is a distinctiveness (and I don"t mean uniqueness) about the Indian leader — how he thinks, feels, and behaves at the workplace." The spiritual gurus of recent times, including Swami Vivekananda, Srila Prabhupada, Ramakrishna Paramhansa, and Sadhguru, have been inspiring millions of mortals to realize their true selves. I have been following these gurus lessons as it creates positivity and clarity among your thoughts. As Sadhguru says, "Spirituality has nothing to do with the atmosphere you live in. It is about the atmosphere you create within yourself."

I love reading these books and applying these principles in my day-to-day life. They help me a lot in focusing on right priorities and objectives, self-awareness, having a different point of view, and listening to others' opinions. While Western leadership principles focus on problem-solving and goal orientation, Hindu philosophy emphasizes dharma (path to rightness), selflessness, and fair-mindedness. In the *Bhagavad Gita*, another important text, Lord Krishna prescribes dutiful action as doing one's duty diligently without being overly attached to actions and not inordinately motivated by results. This insight believes that actions are in one's hands but results are not, and it emphasizes that no progress is linear. These lessons helped me in my leadership style to support the right practices and have ethical behavior in place. I enabled my teams to do their best, and that brought innovation in the workplace. We built large complex digital solutions for our clients. We even achieved the highest points on customer satisfaction surveys for multiple years.

Indian culture has many texts and manuscripts providing nuggets of inspiration and wisdom. Another example is the Upanishads, two hundred-odd manuscripts crowdsourced over centuries. Arthur Schopenhauer titled them "the highest human wisdom." One of my favorite quotes from the Upanishads is, "You are what your deep, driving desire is. As your desire is, so is your will. As your will is, so is your deed. As your deed is, so is your destiny." This is the best definition of luck I have encountered. This quote is relevant today when venture capitalists evaluate management teams of early-stage investments. In the face of intense competitive uncertainty, this innate "deep, driving desire" is what venture capitalists look for.

Vedanta philosophy, which is central to Hindu thought, provides an elegant perspective for those stuck in dilemmas. Understanding the concept of *Maya* provides organizations with one way to grow beyond their current limitations in addressing complexity, fostering creativity, and increasing effectiveness.

Life is strange, but life leads to epiphanies, too, on so many occasions. You could give up all hope, but life itself will teach you the power of keeping the faith in one striking moment. Of never giving up. Of finding strength through people's actions and words. That might lead you to believe in spirituality since that stroke of luck is nothing short of a spiritual awakening.

How can we have faith, keep from giving up or getting pulled down, and handle complex situations? The answer lies in spirituality.

Early in my career, I used to work long hours to make sure I fixed urgent problems to make sure business ran smoothly and to not lose any revenue. There were situations when my efforts were underappreciated. Still, I always tried to motivate myself by believing that working hard always paid off. I always focused on learning more and taking up new challenges. I took on new leadership roles leading large global teams, digital initiatives, practices, and an ePMO or doing enterprise-wide agile transformation.

Problems and challenges are always there. But when we are in the right frame of mind, we can come together to find solutions and move ahead. We are often looking for someone else to solve the problem, some hero or some other person. But we need to become the change and lead. As a leader, what significance does spirituality hold? If we define it on a basic level, leadership is a process whereby an individual influences a group of individuals to achieve a common goal. This working dimension is a starting dimension, and there are many dimensions to leadership.

Combining spirit and leadership suggests that the leader who incorporates spirituality into their leadership will cause others to seek out and understand their inner selves and foster a sense of meaning and significance among their followers. In other words, they will seek a holistic approach to leadership in which the leader emphasizes an understanding of significance and interconnectedness among employees. This also enables trust and transparency among employees and teams.

Applying spiritual values and principles to the workplace has many benefits. It is very important to understand the importance of employees finding meaning in their work. Spirituality, for me, is embracing the deepest values and meanings by which I live. What is my purpose? What are my core values? Knowing your purpose and meaning are widely recognized as essential to human flourishing, making spirituality increasingly acceptable as a dimension of many in the workplace, including leaders.

These fundamental questions, when addressed in the workplace, help in finding meaning in work. It creates a true community workplace that consists of people with shared traditions, values, and beliefs. The focus should be on:

- people, and not position and power;
- transformation and diversity, and not conformity; and
- partnership, collaboration, and inspiration, and not control.

Contrary to popular belief, spirituality in leadership does not require that the leader adheres to a particular religion or attempt to convince subordinates to pursue a specific set of religious principles. It is more concerned with the development of employees as people first—people who exhibit compassion to other employees, superiors, subordinates, and customers. The spiritual element is not necessarily connected to any world religion but occurs independently as an expression of humanity. Spirituality is a quality that stands alongside the emotional, intellectual, and physical aspects of a human being.

The definition of the modern workplace has changed. It is not just a place where people work but also a place where they form friendships, socialize, and attempt to find a sense of fulfillment. It is also a place where people try to derive meaning from the activities that comprise "work" and how these activities fit within the greater fabric of individuals' lives. My spiritual side helped me understand this meaning in the early days of my career and since then, I have been promoting building a culture of collaboration, learning, and innovation. It starts with mentoring and guiding teams/people around trust, transparency, collaboration, agility, and intrinsic motivation. Also, as more and more people care about their personal work–life balance, individual satisfaction in work and in life has become more important. This quest for meaning has prompted the recognition that spirituality in the workplace and spiritual leadership are real issues affecting the quality of life in modern organizations.

Having compassion toward others and experiencing a mindful inner consciousness in the pursuit of meaningful work enables transcendence. Spiritual leadership comprises three principal components:

vision, hope/faith, and selfless love. These convert to a leader's values, attitudes, and behaviors, respectively.

COVID-19 has prompted us to reflect deeper on the role of spirituality in leadership. The last three decades have seen an increased awareness of spirituality. Many have decided to take up meditation, mindfulness, and other spiritual practices to help them cope with unprecedented uncertainty and stress.

Therefore, spirituality and spiritual practices play a key role in helping leaders be more effective in several ways. It can be seen as a source of leadership motivation or as a source of ethical grounding leading to virtuous behavior. This naturally leads to further self-knowledge and, ultimately, self-acceptance. It also helps in coping with difficulty and toxicity in the workplace. The ability to reflect and the development of self-awareness as two of the three fundamental building blocks to effective leadership (the third is to have a systematic approach).

Let's turn to Abraham Maslow, the famous American psychologist and inventor of the Hierarchy of Needs. We can see how spirituality plays a role in fulfilling the needs at the higher levels of the hierarchy. According to Maslow's theory, when the needs at the first level of the scale are met, we seek to fulfill the needs on the next level, and so on. After fulfilling physiological, safety, social, and self-esteem needs, we seek self-actualization and self-transcendence needs.

Most leadership development programs respond to the desire to fulfill the need for self-actualization. Leaders are given tools and strategies to: develop self-esteem, self-awareness, and self-discipline; uncover their potential and their purpose; and find the motivation to achieve their goals. Initially, self-actualization was the highest level of development in Maslow's Hierarchy of Needs.

Ethics and Spirituality

In a study of 260 advertising CEOs in Thailand, Phattanacheewapul and Ussahawanitchakit (2009) found a relationship between spirituality and ethics. This study considered spirituality and ethics from an organizational perspective. They defined organizational spirituality mindset (OSM) as a combination of four variables: (1) career obligation; (2) success concentration; (3) sense of ownership; and (4) tasks perseverance. Regression analysis found that virtue ethics had an impact on each of the four dimensions of OSM. The authors concluded that firms with more robust virtue ethics will not only display greater organizational spirituality but will likely be more successful.

Companies can cultivate spiritual practices in the workplace in many ways. There are four principles companies could use at their workplaces:

(1) The organization provides its employees with interesting work processes to learn and develop their competence.

(2) The organization provides meaningful work.

(3) The organization establishes significant social relationships among coworkers.

(4) The employees are trained to live, as human beings, an "integrated life."

Spirituality helped me behave ethically, have passion, gratitude, and empathy, make the right decisions, find meaning in my goals and objectives, challenge myself, and, most importantly, give back to people and communities. Give it a try, and it can help you as well.

About the Author

RISHI KUMAR

Man of Excellence 2021, India Achievers award winner from the Indian Achievers Forum for outstanding professional achievements and contribution to nation-building, Rishi Kumar excels as a seasoned executive working as associate vice president with a multi-national technology service company named Pactera EDGE. He is an executive advisor, transformation strategist, and global speaker with over sixteen years of industry experience focusing on business, digital, and enterprise-wide agile transformation—Rishi mentors and coaches leaders in large organizations and startups alike.

With his thought leadership and commitment to customer-centricity, he has helped multiple Fortune 100 companies in their digital transformation journey, helping them to digitally reinvent themselves, enhance enterprise agility, business insight, increase revenue, and build operational excellence.

He has worked with clients like Walmart Inc, Sears Holding, TJX Companies, Cigna Inc, CVS Health, Boots the Chemist, Florida Power & Light, Royal Bank of Scotland, Michelin, Mapfre Insurance, American Family Insurance, to name a few.

Rishi also advocates building a culture of learning, sharing, and innovation. After spending his time in the UK and India, he moved to the United States in 2013 and resided with his family in Bentonville, Arkansas. He is an exceptionally involved people person, an inclusive leader, and a life-long learner. He also practices spiritual practices and experiences with Vaastu Science, Vedic Science, and Numerology.

Rishi has been contributing, giving back to society, and enabling people since 2006 with many initiatives.

LinkedIn: https://www.linkedin.com/in/contactrishi/
Website: https://rishhikumar.com/

SEVEN

Katy Lumsden

STILL HERE

In the deeps are the violence and terror of which psychology has warned us. But if you ride these monsters down, if you drop with them farther over the world's rim, you find what our sciences cannot locate or name, the substrate, the ocean or matrix or ether which buoys the rest, which gives goodness its power for good, and evil its power for evil, the unified field: our complex and inexplicable caring for each other, and for our life together here. This is given. It is not learned. (Dillard, 2017)

It's surprising what can be seen in the dark, given long enough for vision and cognition to realign. The umbral depths of mental illness revealed unanticipated vibrancy—and irony: this was not the still, empty place for disappearing unnoticed; it was alive with antithesis to my every assumption. What I found was interconnection, self, and a most unexpected route to leadership. But to start to see it, I had to accept a gift.

The sinking was slow and quiet. It came after the thrashing around, my uncustomary attracting of attention to an unfolding disaster. The disaster was mine. The disaster was me. I watched myself, over days, submerge, sink, with a slow grace that was an affront to the violent damage that had scuttled me.

Six weeks after the birth of my daughter, my apotheosis as woman, and I wanted so much to die. But more. Obliteration. Not just to disappear but never to have been here.

Postpartum depression has a particular savagery. I felt complicit in setting myself up for it, by expecting; believing. The word we use as a synonym for being pregnant—*expecting*—binds us to culture and dominion. To losing autonomy. And if one *expects* too much, to losing self. Depression had never been as silent, in my experience, or with so few spectators, as this. Everyone else *expected* too, and the power of confirmation bias hazed sight and dulled sound.

I have lived most of my life looking in at myself. From early on I became very astute at understanding the patterns of other people's behaviour and intuiting what they were likely to need, expect, next. This allowed me to function without expressing my needs and expectations; actually, it enabled me to ignore them. In therapy in my twenties, a decade before this horrifying postpartum terrain, I had described feeling 'pixelated', to the extent that I believed I might at any moment disintegrate into tiny particulates and disappear. During the deepest period of depression at that time, I had held a perception of myself as having a head but no body. Earlier still, in my teens, I had developed a contorting belief that all my thoughts appeared in cartoon-like bubbles over my head, visible to everyone. This anxiety needed no sustenance other than itself. I constantly monitored a logic-defying radar of thoughts, to catch them before I thought them, so that I could edit them and present a curated narrative.

Now, postpartum, I could not reconcile myself to the weight of expectation. Having been very effective in dismantling the usual routes of their expression, I was confronted by insurmountable, irreconcilable needs. Socially unacceptable ones. Following Newtonian mechanics, the reactive force was equal and opposite.

Watching. Sinking. Stilling. The peace of the absence of judgement and action.

And then. In the viscous darkness, there was not obliteration, but God; sitting there, right at the bottom. Waiting. With a joy and tenderness more heartfelt than I have ever known, God said, "At last, we can meet properly." God said, "You think you have no strength, nothing to give, but *this* is all I ask: take; eat."

On the day before the silent sinking began, in the thrashing-around phase, I had sought an intervention which had involved my panicked general practitioner. I couldn't assure her that I wouldn't try to die; but at the end of that day, feeling a little returned from a place beyond, I phoned my mother. "I'm still here," I said.

The work began. This was not a 'pick up your mat and walk' moment. It took me to the other side of action. *I* did not have to act; I had only to accept, and to survive.

Impactful Absence

I realise this might not offer a promising start for insights into leadership. This kind of survival seems inadequately possessing of the action, dynamism, positivity, and directive qualities I would have recognised as leadership then, had I considered it at all. Leadership would have seemed to me an outward-looking role; more the ability to look in on other people than to look in on self.

I had long felt the wrong way out, believing my raw inner landscape to be not only unacceptable but also entirely visible to everyone else. It lacked any cover or respite. The head with no body. Someone recently said that they experienced my lack of sense of self as very controlling, and I've been thinking about that a great deal. I had thought that such an absence of sense of self was insular, isolating, negating. However, considering it now, I can see that I related myself entirely to others, constantly adjusting to their constant adjustments, anticipating, readying. Not apart from everyone else, but a part of everyone else, a kind of unknowing parasitism. My opinions, their opinions; my needs, their needs. Being in the right shape at the right time.

The thing about sinking to the bottom of that dark, liquid place was that there was no rest there, either. Fathoms deep, and this place was vibrant with ways of being that had adapted. And alive with irony. It was the nourishment of challenge that was being offered. Knowing me far better than I did, my Creator knew I could not resist that. "Try it," God said, "Taste it."

The challenge lay in having no context of others; in relocating, uprooting, to self. I picture the ascent from that place like rock climbing: looking for footholds; trying them out; slipping; sinking; starting again.

I did it. I fucking did it. For two years survival was not a day-by-day, break-it-down thing. It was clawing and crawling my way through each minute of each one of those days. I drew energy from the provisioning of challenge. At the same time, I fought it. I hated it for its unfamiliarity, and because it fed me. It took away all my moorings and bearings; and I resented the gift of it. It gave no option other than to be with myself.

Then, one day, I realised I had not marked each minute, that my sight had been set somewhere other than the relentlessness of surviving the last and steeling myself for the next. There had been some relief; tiny moments, but there, nonetheless. That was like staring from underneath at the surface of the water.

Baptism: An Exit Strategy

I had been asked to speak at a baptism months before. I did so reflecting on the baptism of my daughter. I had deliberated a great deal ahead of her baptism, read widely, considered deeply. I had thought about the story of Jesus' baptism, his immersion in the Jordan River. The word baptism is derived from a Greek word meaning "to dip", and it had struck me that while attention tends to be drawn to the 'going in', in a way it is the 'coming out' that is the crucial part, though, of course, it is contingent on the first having occurred.

As he emerged from the water, it is recounted that the Spirit descended on Jesus and he was named and claimed by God as his beloved son. To my mind, there is something significant in the fact that this happened not as Jesus was about to go into the water, or even while he was in it, but as he came out again. The first thing anyone would do having been immersed would be to gasp for breath, and I think it interesting that, returning to the Greeks, the word for breath is interconnected with the word for spirit. Breathing in new life and promise, a body being filled with spirit as with breath. I had listened to a sermon in church soon after my daughter was born in which our minister spoke of baptism as a kind of uncovering. She spoke of an emerging, a revealing that leaves us free to tell the truth about our presence in the world (Meyer, 2012).

It has been ten years since my daughter's difficult arrival in the world and eight since I stared at the sunlight and sky from underneath the surface of the water. The years since have felt like a huge gasp for breath, propelling out and up.

Filling with breath, filling with spirit. Filling with presence.

In finding and testing those footholds, I began to pay attention to those callings or motivations that drew me forwards, curious. It was one such that had brought me to Ireland from Scotland in my teens to study, and that had led to my first freelancing jobs in calligraphy and design, which became my first career. But now I was compelled towards people at the interface of vulnerabilities—serving, ministering. I found reserves for learning I hadn't known in myself; and a brass-necked cheek in asking my organisation to pivot me into a human resources role they had no idea I had interest in, never mind any skill or talent. God knew: the nourishment of challenge. Facing myself, fears, insecurities, was compelling. I found I relished new tests, because they gave me new insights, new footholds. And from there new horizons presented; and I went back to school. Postgraduate work in organisational behaviour and organisational development expanded my knowledge. But more: the introvert had to engage, with others and with self. I was welcomed, challenged, nourished. Still gasping for breath. Coaching was formative, allowing a clear set of values to emerge which I know I have worked to all my life but which now I could discern and name. Meeting myself in this way gave more footholds and a sense of myself which, in my fifth decade, have given me somewhere to stand out of the water, breath steadying.

This understanding of self and presence has been the most important, necessary work of my life. It has also, in some respects, provided great discomfort as those things that had accumulated to support my functioning without either must be re-examined.

Interconnect and Innovate

My most recent work for a postgraduate qualification in organisational development has brought my work and practice into alignment with my sense of something greater than the self; and I realise this has been possible precisely *because* of a sense and understanding of self. My research led me to the work of Franklyn and Maura Sills in Core Process Psychotherapy and their use of the Buddhist concept of *interbeing* (Sills, 2009, p. xiv). In parallel I was exploring James Gleick's work on Chaos Theory and its exhilarating proposition that through *interbeing* we are constantly interacting, aligning, absorbing. Generating and regenerating. I considered whether this was the place I had been in before, the pixelating one. However, I felt that it differed in the most fundamental way: for this interaction to be effective and healthy, it requires a meridian, a place of substance and self-understanding. One which is not static but understood and acknowledged. Peggy Holman describes this interaction facilitating our "capacity to adapt, to engage the unexpected, to be our unique, authentic selves, inviting others to do the same…generating novelty and innovation" (Holman, 2015, p. 147). This seemed, suddenly, the essence of leadership.

Early in my return to study, surrounded by elevated experience and superlatives, I had caught sight of leadership which in some senses met my former, unthinking, construct of what a leader is and does; but it had also caught me unawares—moved me to tears, in truth—and I wanted to know why. I had recognised something in it that transcended that action-driven, directive trope.

When I encountered Peggy Holman's description, I understood.

The resonance was enhanced because I could acknowledge that, over the formative journey I had undertaken, I had acquired some sense of my own "unique, authentic self" (Holman, 2015, p. 147). Now, a glimpse of the interactive potential between individuals, creating flourishing, optimal people, organisations, and societies, gave a vista of possibilities and power beyond imagining. I was intrigued, thrilled, by the realisation that this was not only possible, theoretical, but happening. What moved me most was the idea that this was unstoppable; that this kind of congruence and alignment was happening unbidden, and to allow it to work to its most full transformative capability what was needed was…well…nothing. But this was not the 'nothing' of obliteration; this was the 'nothing' of observing; accepting; of the place beyond action; the challenge of 'take; eat'.

The imperative is that a sense of self is foundational: crucial, but not the destination; rather the starting-point for the greater voyage which allows self not just to exist but also to contribute and serve through interconnection. In this sense, to exist is to impact. In itself, this is neutral. If self-awareness and intentionality are brought to this, leadership of the type Holman describes becomes not just possible but inevitable. Drawing again on themes of mechanics, this seems a paradigm of quantum leadership, leaving the Newtonian, straight-line concepts of human interaction standing.

In the quantum universe, we cannot predict and control. We can only accept. This is not a giving-up or a disengagement. It requires the constant and deep work of finding and recognising our meridian as it is transformed by our openness.

Lose Control—and Lead

By strange synchronicity, in church this morning our minister again spoke of baptism while reflecting on part of Paul's letter to the people of Ephesus. It washes away any entitlement to certainty, she observed, as we bring the darkness of our immersion with us; but it gives light enough for our hearts to see by (Meyer, 2021). Her exegesis brought me to the core of this quantum kind of leadership. Its dynamism comes from acceptance of uncertainty and from recognising the growth inherent in relating ambiguity to self; to letting the heart see.

To say that my leadership practice has been transformed sounds grandiose and suggestive of some great sense of purpose that was never there. I never sought 'leadership'; but finding those footholds of presence and self has led me beyond self. What I found when I could sink no further, and what I have called God, may be what others recognise as the place of *interbeing* and universal, quantum, connection; Dillard's "substrate…which buoys the rest" (Dillard, 2017). In that place, with the constant work of attentiveness to self and acceptance of uncertainty, leadership cannot help but manifest.

In this context, the words of Dutch theologian Henri Nouwen become a kind of summary of a calling to leadership: "Jesus' invitation," he describes, "is a call to abandon relational safety zones and become vulnerable, independent, and obedient to the voice of unconditional love. It implies living gratefully and finding an intimate solidarity with brothers and sisters in the human family" (Nouwen, 2009, p79). But this kind of *interbeing* can produce leadership only if the self is readied and understood. In the Christian setting, this has brought me back with new eyes to Jesus' response to the Pharisees that makes loving neighbour and loving self contingent on each other, as recorded in the Gospels of Matthew (22:39) and Mark (12:31). As so often, Jesus draws on wisdom and exhortation from the Hebrew texts his audiences would have known by heart; the books of Deuteronomy and Leviticus, for example, contain similar instruction. But as always, Jesus responds to the

Pharisees with the twist of the Covenant of the New Testament. Far from being an expression of subservience or sublimation of self, the humour and subversion in this, and the ferocity, is the call to a place beyond action and of transformation through interconnection. It is the place of Marsha M. Linehan's "radical acceptance" (Linehan, 2020, p. 38): the constant and profound work of being; the challenge of accepting what is given, not learned (Dillard, 2017). Take; eat.

This reminds of the contingency of baptism: the 'coming out' demands a 'going in'. But so much more than this, it requires that we accept this as not just inevitable but necessary for what biblical scholar Walter Wink describes as falling upwards, "into autonomy and consciousness" (Wink, 1992, p. 57). As Jesus gasped from the Jordan, he was given meaning and interconnection beyond self. But he emerged also imbued with baptismal ambiguity. In permitting this for ourselves time and time again, we lead with the intent of Holman's quantum view. Through awareness and acceptance that we do this in a context of interconnection, our work of recalibrating, returning to our meridian, deepens presence and self in a way that transcends ego.

It is instinct to try to claim and control the interconnections: we found them; we changed them; we helped them; we showed them. Nouwen instead invites different possibilities: if we can relinquish this control, "we open ourselves to an unknown future with many surprises" (Nouwen, 2009, pp. 79–80). And, I think, crucially, we facilitate this possibility for each other.

This kind of leadership is not performative, because it is not possessive or acquisitive. It doesn't covet; it loves itself and others in constant equilibrial dependency.

This performative aspect is a default for me, as someone who has spent so long observing outside of self, and it takes vigilance and acceptance—and falling—to keep turning outside in and to be present there. Or held. Held in the promise of interconnection, at the fulcrum of the contingency of interbeing and being. And in understanding that because I exist, I impact, and in not being afraid of it. The delight of the journey ahead of me is to accept that as we each exist we are transformed by interconnection and resonate differently, a limitless constellation of falling stars, each one the light by which the hearts of others see.

I'm still here. A little returned. But now the place beyond, the universe I glimpsed, illuminates each component of that quiet defiance differently according to my constellatory place and the direction of the light, moment by moment. Now it is not a foothold, a place of grip and scrape and shocking effort, but a point for stepping off. Presence is at once complete and never finished.

Leadership is a being word.

References

Dillard, A. (2017), 'Annie Dillard's Classic Essay: "Total Eclipse"', *The Atlantic*, 08 August 2017, available at https://www.theatlantic. com/science/archive/2017/08/annie-dillards-total-eclipse/ 536148/ [accessed 30/08/2021]

Gleick, J. (1984), 'Solving the Mathematical Riddle of Chaos', *New York Times Magazine*, 10 June 1984, available at https://www.nytimes. com/1984/06/10/magazine/solving-the-mathematical-riddle-of-chaos.html [accessed 15/08/2021]

Gleick, J. (1987), *Chaos: Making a New Science*, Viking Penguin Inc, New York, NY, USA

Holman, P. (2015), 'Complexity, Self-Organization, and Emergence', in G. R. Bushe, and R. J. Marshak (eds.), *Dialogic Organization Development: The Theory and Practice of Transformational Change*, Chapter 6, pp. 123–149, Berrett-Koehler Publishers, Inc., Oakland, California

Linehan, M. M. (2020), 'Walking a Tightrope' *Psychology Today*, Vol. 53, No. 1, (Jan/Feb 2020), pp. 36–39.

Meyer, K. P. (2012), *Covenant Service*, 08 January, Christ Church United Presbyterian and Methodist Church, Sandymount, Dublin, Ireland

Meyer, K. P. (2021), *Service of Worship*, 15 August, Christ Church United Presbyterian and Methodist Church, Sandymount, Dublin, Ireland

Nouwen, H. J. M. (2009), *Home Tonight: Further Reflection on the Parable of the Prodigal Son*, Darton, Longman & Todd Ltd., London, UK

Sills, F. (2009), 'Being and Becoming: Psychodynamics, Buddhism, and the Origins of Selfhood', North Atlantic Books, Berkeley, CA, USA

Wink, W. (1992), *Engaging the Powers: Discernment and Resistance in a World of Domination*, Augsberg Fortress, Minneapolis, MN, USA

About the Author

KATY LUMSDEN

Katy Lumsden has been many things and isn't finished yet.

She has been variously ill, depressed, anxious, self-harming, bullied, and exhausted; graphic designer, calligrapher, human resources and organisational development practitioner, learning facilitator, student, parent, spouse, sibling, child, worship leader, elder-elect of the Presbyterian Church in Ireland, church council member, introvert, extrovert, and one of fewer than fifty artists worldwide to have been awarded Craft Membership of the Society of Heraldic Arts. And, indeed, she is still many of these.

In Katy's chapter, she will reveal a very personal story of navigation and sense-making, the journey inwards often unsought but formative and allowing an exhilarating voyage outwards. This has forged connections and alignment which are grounding but compel an onward search for calling and authenticity.

Holding an honours degree in visual communications, post-graduate qualifications in organisational behaviour and organisational development and transformation, and currently working towards an MBS in business practice, Katy is a human resources practitioner with the National Library of Ireland, one of Ireland's foremost cultural institutions. She is also a leadership development facilitator and founder of Know No Bounds, a nascent leadership development facilitation provider with a focus on leadership for children and adolescents; and contributor to congregational life in her United Presbyterian and Methodist church congregation in Dublin.

LinkedIn:
https://linkedin.com/in/katy-lumsden-04508b194

EIGHT

Dr. Tammy Mason

SUCCESS THROUGH SERVANTHOOD IN MY WALK WITH
GOD: EMBRACING SELFLESS GIVING AS THE HEART OF
TRULY LIVING

My entire life and career of over thirty-two years as an educational
and organizational leader, as a servant leader, was shaped by my
faith and belief in God, and how He divinely ordered my steps from
one phase to the next throughout the journey. What does it mean to
be a servant or servant leader? What is meant by servanthood? I
know there are many definitions, perceptions, and opinions
regarding servant leadership. There have been books written on the
subject, research conducted, coaching, and the like. However, what I
have found to be true from my own personal experiences is this—
the passion to serve others selflessly burns deep within me. It's
always with me. As a servant leader, I have an internal flame that
never goes out, nor can it be extinguished. Being a servant leader is
not contingent upon me having a title, a position, an office, wealth,
or a certain knowledge or skill set. The beauty of servanthood is it's
a choice, and it meets you right where you are!

I am reminded of the great lessons that Jesus taught the crowds and
His disciples saying, "Let the greatest among you be the servant of
all. For whoever makes himself great shall be humbled and whoever
humbles himself shall be made great" (Matthew 23:11–12).
Throughout life, I worked very hard to do what was right in the eyes

of God and to please others, to a certain degree. But, I never wanted to be great. In fact, I was the one who always sat in the back (and I still do sometimes), cringed whenever my name was called in public, and felt that 911 needed to be dialed if I ever had to publicly receive an award or special recognition!

My best work has always been done from behind the scenes. Even as a philanthropist, I have chosen to keep that work private regarding what specific individuals, families, businesses, and organizations I choose to support and work with. I feel my clients deserve that, although they often want to share with others the blessings they have received. I also believe that there are certain elements or characteristics that should accompany servant leadership, such as compassion, empathy, positivity, encouragement, being able to easily connect with others, a giving spirit, transparency, selflessness, putting others' needs before your own—basically, walking in humility. Being a servant leader is true humility in action. Early on, my mantra quickly became, "How can I help?" and "What do you need?"

An Early Calling

There is a saying that seeing is believing. Well, I have a saying that *hearing is believing*. When I was five years old, I remember hearing God's voice for the very first time. Only then, I did not know that it was God's voice or Him trying to speak to my spirit. However, what was said to me changed the course of my entire life. I remember exactly where I was when I experienced it. I have five siblings, and four of us had just gotten off the bus at our stop and were walking home. We lived on a long dirt road. I was running ahead of everyone else and had managed to create quite a bit of distance between us. That's when it happened. It stopped me cold in my tracks. The main thing God impressed upon my heart was that I was being set apart, I would be different, and I would not follow the crowd. I would not go the way of the world. It almost seemed as if it was a warning of some sort. It was surreal. I found it quite intriguing, and I carried it in my heart every single day from that point on.

In fact, my routine became attempting to be the first one off the bus everyday so I could run ahead of my siblings and, hopefully, hear "that voice" again. That was pretty heavy stuff for a shy, five-year-old, introverted little girl to carry around. But maybe, just maybe, God knew that even at five years old, I was wise beyond my years.

Teen Years Transformation

As I fast forward to my teen years, it was clearly evident that God had "marked" me for sure. I never desired to engage in any of the activities that some teenagers do—like going to parties or dances, experimental drinking, or smoking. Instead, I stayed home, studied, or watched television. I had not forgotten "that voice" that was guiding me. It was forever etched in my mind and spirit. This is where the pieces began to come together for me. While we, as a family, were attending church every Sunday, (and I was a "good girl") I did not have a personal relationship with the Lord. Realizing that there was something deeper and more intimate that I needed to tap into, I gave my heart and life to Jesus on August 31, 1983, as a teenager, and I never looked back.

It happened during a summer revival crusade that my mom wanted us to attend. Initially, I was fearful and didn't really want to go because I didn't know what to expect. I remember it being on a school night (Wednesday). The crusade was held in an elementary school gymnasium, and at the end of the service, my older sister and I walked up front to be prayed for publicly to receive Christ (according to John 3:3–7; Romans 10:9–10; and 1 John 1:9). There were several others who also came forward for prayer. I remember being so nervous at first. But, after we prayed with the pastor, I felt so much better. There were others who gathered around us and laid hands on our shoulders as we prayed to the Lord, then swarmed us with hugs in celebration of our salvation. Now, I could see and feel the difference. The wheels began to turn. This was a turning point indeed, for it quickly catapulted me into my purpose, my calling, my desire to serve others.

Servanthood Bootcamp

One of the first things we did as a family was transition from our current place of worship to a new church that better suited our spiritual needs. This decision, once again, proved to be life-changing. My now late pastor became one of the greatest mentors and the most influential person in my life, a surrogate father. My father was no longer in my life at that time. When I look at the woman I have become today, I know that it is because of the time Pastor Vehe took in taking me under his wings, mentoring me, training me, and just pouring into my life.

Pastor Vehe was a highly intelligent and gifted man who had a very unique story of his own. He was an architect, graphic artist, businessman, writer, and financial expert. Originally from Ghana, West Africa, he came to the United States after hearing God's voice instructing him to do so. He taught me how to walk with God and what it really means to serve. Pastor Vehe saw talent, skills, and potential in me that no one else had yet recognized.

I recall a few times when he and his wife would attend out-of-town conferences. I was asked to stay in their home and babysit their children. I helped clean the church bathrooms and vacuum the church offices. Little by little, as I was faithful in the small things, more opportunities came. The Bible says that he who is faithful in little is also faithful in much (Luke 16:10).

From that point, I was asked to join the church choir and work with the youth. After serving faithfully in those capacities, I was promoted to Christian Education Director, whereby I established and coordinated all educational programs in the church—including Vacation Bible School, Children's Church, Sunday School, and Summer Youth Camp. In 1992, I was invited to come on board as the staff secretary in the church office, alongside the church secretary and treasurer. As I continued to serve faithfully in all areas, I was appointed as a singles ministry leader, women's fellowship leader, worship arts praise dance team, home cell group leader, follow-up team coordinator, TV floor director, and television/camera crew member for our television ministry network. Finally, as a result of my faithfulness, I was invited to join the Board of Directors. I cannot express how much joy I found in serving!

By this time, I had graduated college with honors and secured my first teaching job right before I graduated college. God hand-picked me for three available teaching positions, and I got to choose the one I wanted. As I began my career in education, I somehow still managed to continue serving in the various roles at the church. I would arrive at the church office directly after school or work and volunteer my time until around 9:00 p.m. each day, and Saturday mornings until about noon, along with two other staff members. The amazing thing is I never felt tired, exhausted, or burned out. My spiritual engine never ran out of fuel! The more I served, the more I wanted to serve. There was a desire present to help out in any way I could. That desire was always at the forefront. At the same time, little did I know that this experience was preparing me for what was to come in school leadership. As I worked with my pastor for many years, I acquired stellar graphic design skills for producing newsletters, bulletins, brochures, and various other promotional and marketing materials, and a skill set range that was second to none.

As I worked on advanced degrees, God brought other mentors into my life, which opened the doors of opportunity for me even wider. God even opened some doors I had not knocked on! And for doors that seemed closed, He nudged me to push a little harder. They were just closed, not locked!

Preparation Meets Opportunity

I loved teaching and working with children of all ages! I was such a natural at it and highly creative. In fact, I received the Teacher-of-the-Year award during my second year of teaching, which had never happened in that school or district before! Now, as a general rule, one has to teach a minimum of three years to even be nominated. I taught second graders (ages seven to eight), which I thought was the perfect age. They were old enough to do some things on their own, but young enough that they still wanted to be hugged and loved on. I loved my students as if they were my own children. Once a year, we would take a field trip to my mom's house on a Saturday, before the school year ended, to have a cook-out, jump rope, hula hoop, and play games in the yard. Yes, we could actually do things like that back then simply with parent permission letters. Additionally, I taught third, fourth, and fifth graders later on. In my mind, I thought I would teach forever. I wasn't pursuing a move or career in organizational leadership or administration. However, it came looking for me.

After teaching for about fifteen years, I was approached by the superintendent at the end of the school year in 2003. He came to my classroom on the last day of school and asked me if I would consider moving to another school in the district to pursue an assistant principal position. He explained to me that because of my leadership ability in the local organizations and many areas, I would be a good prospect for this job. He also told me that I was already prepared by having my certification in leadership. No one else had that particular degree or licensure at the other school. It seemed like a no-brainer; however, I wanted to be 100% sure, so I told him I would need to pray about it and get back with him. Basically, I spent most of the summer praying about the situation, and I finally decided to take the offer. I served in that role as assistant principal for about seven years. It was not easy, and I faced many obstacles along the way. But through it all, God was faithful to keep His promises.

Purpose in My Pain

Do you remember that student in any of your classes that the teacher just did not seem to like, no matter what he or she did to find favor with the teacher? Maybe you were that student. Well, I was that assistant principal. I felt I was often mistreated for no reason, and I never could understand why. No matter what I did, how hard I worked, and how professional I was, the principal just did not care for me. I knew it was a test of my faith, my character, and no matter what, truth and righteousness would prevail over the forces of darkness.

I went through some dark days, many times feeling alone like I had no one to talk to about the situation. I remember wanting to leave that job so many times. In fact, I did try to leave after my first year there. I resigned and planned to take a full-time assistant professor position that I had been offered at Emmanuel College. The day before signing that contract, I did not have one hundred percent peace about it. I called the dean, thanked him for the opportunity, apologized for backing out, and explained that I felt the timing was a bit off. Then, I called the superintendent. He said no action had yet been taken on my resignation letter, so I was free to return to my assistant principal position if that was what I wanted to do.

Little did I know there would be a price to pay. Retaliation. More mistreatment. What was I thinking by coming back? God had a plan. I knew He did. There was a lesson in there somewhere. I just had to get through this season to see the good in this. And sure enough, things got much worse. I went through so much. This went on for seven long years. I applied for other jobs in every neighboring county. Every door continued to close…and then locked! How could this be? Why was this happening? Why could I not leave? In that seven-year wilderness experience, I began to do something I had never done before. I began to fast and pray during my lunch break. I would go into my office, kneel in the bathroom, and pray instead of eating my lunch. Many days, I felt the hot tears run down my face as I crouched in the corner of that tiny bathroom. I would stay there until I felt God blanket me with His peace.

I continued to do my job well, but it still wasn't enough. I felt a strong dislike toward me. It was a relentless pursuit. Then, one day, I began to feel less bothered. And, eventually, I was not bothered at all. I was always kind and professional to this person. All of a sudden, I saw something shift. Even though the situation or person had not changed, I changed how I responded to the situation. At the end of seven years, the individual vacated that position! It happened abruptly. So, I asked God what was the purpose of all that happening? He gave me three specific things. Here are the lessons:

1. He allowed me to experience this harshness so I could see what kind of leader I did *not* want to be.

2. He wanted me to develop compassion for those I come in contact with. Because I was hurting, He wanted me to experience that pain so I could extend compassion to other hurting people.

3. He wanted me to respond in genuineness, kindness, and love—not out of necessity or requirement, but until I could no longer feel the pain. In other words, until it didn't bother me anymore. No matter what was going on around me, I still needed to be able to serve others and do my job well, even in the midst of total chaos and pain. I was still on a mission.

So, needless to say, I passed that test! Sometimes, there is pain in your purpose and a purpose *within* your purpose. Promotion comes *after* you pass the test.

It's a Man's World...Or Is It?

When I entered the teaching profession, over three decades ago, being a principal was a male-dominated position. So, getting my first principal's job was not as easy as I thought it would be. Unfortunately, at that time, those positions were being recycled through what is known as "the good old boy system". In the past, it had been customary for an assistant principal to be promoted to principal in the school whenever there was a vacancy. However, when I got to the door, the rules suddenly changed. I was told that I would have to interview for the position, even though I had been the only assistant principal in the school for over seven years. Imagine that. Was it because I was black, female, or both? So, I interviewed for the principalship. Still, that wasn't enough. No one else had applied for the position. I was the "Lone Ranger" applicant. Out of respect for me, no one else (my colleagues in leadership) applied for the position. They knew that I had earned the right to move up as principal in that school. However, the newly appointed superintendent, who was a friend of the former principal, asked someone else (who was not interested in the position) to apply for the job. The job was held up for over two weeks due to this underhanded conspiracy. The other person did apply, but I still got the job. Long story short…what God has for you is only for *you*. It cannot be taken away, and no one else can have your blessing if your name is already on it! For promotion comes from God (Psalm 75:6–7). Once I was in, God let me know that I was there to stay. I had been granted a special assignment. His plan and purpose for me was to serve others in that capacity to the best of my ability. And that I did. God rewards faithfulness. It did not matter which school I was assigned to or asked to be the principal of. I excelled in all areas. Learn to be the person who can shine from under a rock if you have to.

Timing Is Everything

When I was younger, I had a fear of heights, and I still do to a certain extent. I remember one scorching hot summer, during the Fourth of July week, my family and I traveled to Texas to visit my brother, Kenneth, and his family. While showing us around, he took us to the mall. Now, I don't know who invented the escalator, but that was something I always dreaded getting on—because there's nothing worse than being afraid of heights while moving at the same time. However, one important thing I noticed that helped to ease my fears was getting the timing down of when to step on the escalator. It had to be just right. Once I figured that out, it was no longer a fear.

So it is when a critical decision needs to be made. When God speaks to my heart about a matter, there is a distinct window of opportunity that awaits. It is imperative that I am decisive, in synchronization with the nuggets of wisdom that God has spoken to my heart and mind, and that I move in step with Him. Not running ahead, nor lagging behind. I must move precisely at the right moment. So, how does one balance this?

When I was considering retiring about three years ago, I did not
have a set time in mind. When people would ask me when I was
going to retire, I would say things like: "I am not quite ready yet";
"maybe in a couple of years"; or "it's getting closer and closer." The
simple truth was that I did not know because I had not consulted
with God on the *timing* of the matter. Of course, I had spent time
praying about it, and others were also praying for me. But, I did not
have the specifics.

I had entertained the strong possibility of retirement in December
2020, January 2021, or the end of the school year, June 2021.
However, one late September afternoon as I was headed home from
a meeting, I felt God nudge me, "What difference will two more
months make, when you can retire *whenever* you want?" The ball was
in my court for sure! I wasn't working out of necessity. I was there
for ministry purposes—to serve and to impact lives. Then, I heard
clearly, October 1st. There was a Dollar General store on my right
as I rounded the corner. I pulled into the parking lot and sat for a
minute. I thought, *Really, God? Can we do this? Yes, I can!* I immediately
felt God's overwhelming peace and joy come over me like a flood. I
got back on the road and rushed home.

As soon as I arrived home, I ran upstairs to my office, made a
couple quick phone calls, and wrote my official letter of retirement
to the superintendent. I was so excited! Feeling quite giddy, actually.
I wanted to keep it to myself until the deal was done. I love a little
element of surprise! That Saturday, September 26, 2020, I went by
the school, and we packed up my office. Just like that. On Sunday
night, September 27, I sent my letter of retirement to the superintendent. I contacted my teachers and staff. I had already held
several conversations with them previously that the time was getting
near. On Thursday morning, October 1, 2020, I was home...and
officially retired! I was relaxed and sitting in my sunroom, legs
crossed, reading, and watching ten beautiful geese and an egret have
a party down at the lake! The sneaky smile I had on my face
—priceless!

I walked away from it all, at the drop of a hat, because the Lord said it was time. My mission had been completed. Never looked back. Never wondered if I made the right decision. Never questioned God. He did the rest! Had I waited another year, month, week, or even a day, the trajectory of my life could have been changed forever. I could have been walking outside of God's perfect will for my life. So, yes, timing is everything. God's part was laying out the plan of next steps for my life. My part was to act on it. And, I made sure that everything in my life aligned with the October 1st date He dropped in my spirit. I did not want to miss that window of opportunity. Now, the Lord is ushering me into a new season in which I get to serve so many more people—now on a global level, not just locally. I am thrilled over what is taking place in my life right now and what is on the horizon!

Final Curtain Call

My faith in God is the cornerstone of everything I am today and all I have accomplished. Being able to sit quietly, reflect, and hear God speak to my heart has provided direction, guidance, and everything I needed to be successful in life, as well as walking in my true purpose and calling as a servant leader. It took me a while to learn that God is *always* speaking, but are we in a position to hear Him? Do we even really want to hear Him because what He has to say may not always be what we want to hear? Are we busy doing all the talking?

Looking back, those experiences were some of the best days of my life. God set it up in such a way that I became the principal of several schools where the student population consisted primarily of high poverty, at-risk students—even some juveniles who were already caught up in the court system. And, I absolutely loved it! I fell in love with the students, their families, and my teachers and staff. One thing about it for sure—you cannot take the desire to serve others out of someone. That's what I felt set me apart from so many others. No one could wipe this radiant smile off my face! Yes, there were some "not-so-good" moments along the way, but what was on the inside of me could not be shaken. God's Spirit in me was solid, firm, and very present. When God spoke to my heart at five years old, He knew that I would heed the call.

There is a collage of photos of me with my family, and from my school years, that hangs on the wall in my foyer. Occasionally, when I walk through, I will pause to look at them. As I closely lean in to look at the one of sweet little Tammy, I can clearly see in her eyes the shyness, the timidity, the innocence, the desire to please others, the feeling of not quite being good enough, the longing to be loved for who she is, and the wonderment of who she will become some-day. If I could tell that young, impressionable sweet soul anything at all, it would be this: just relax, trust God in all things, and fully rely on Him because He loves you unconditionally, and He has your life and plans in His very hands. God's got this, and He has you! And, one day, you will be walking out God's plan and purpose for your life through service to others.

So, now I get to be the CEO of my life moving forward! It's the most incredible, liberating feeling that just cannot be put into words. I have to pinch myself some days to make sure this is real, that I get to enjoy this kind of life. I am not working to build someone else's dream; I've built my own. I get to plan my days, appointments, meetings with clients, travel, extended devotionals and meditation, whatever…how I spend my time, and who I choose to spend it with. More time for writing, reflecting, exercise, wellness, self-care, you name it. What could be greater than this? All because God chose to speak to the heart of a five-year-old, timid little country girl who was just minding her own business and being a child. But, He knew I would be able to feel and sense His presence in that very moment, take heed, and walk out His plan and purpose for my life, through service to others, under the guidance and direction of the Holy Spirit. Everything has worked out exactly the way it should for me, according to Romans 8:28. I am so excited to immerse myself in this next phase of life…unleashing all of my unlimited potential and opportunities, all in the Name of the Lord! Here's to servant leader-ship. Cheers!

About the Author

DR. TAMMY MASON

Newly retired from the corporate world, Dr. Tammy Mason is a strategic philanthropist in the private business sector. Additionally, she serves as an adjunct professor in the School of Education at Emmanuel College, a private Christian college in Georgia, and has been a member of its Advisory Board since 2013. She is the founder and sponsor of the "Women of Destiny" (WOD) college campus ministry that provides spiritual support and guidance to female students and women in the community.

Dr. Mason has spent over three decades as a public school educator —including teacher, assistant principal, school principal at all levels, and director of alternative education. An avid researcher, she has earned five degrees in the areas of early childhood and elementary education, administration and supervision, educational leadership, and curriculum and instruction. Dr. Mason is a long-time member of the National Education Association and the National Society of Leadership and Success.

Dr. Mason's expertise in the public education setting, strong organizational leadership skills, and professional development initiatives has earned her numerous awards and recognition over the years. As a servant leader, she is passionate about supporting causes that are near and dear to her heart.

A proud graduate of Clemson University, Dr. Mason is an avid college football fan and loves attending or watching games with her family and friends as she "coaches" from the sofa on any given Saturday. Go Tigers!

LinkedIn: https://www.linkedin.com/in/dr-tammy-mason-94711b167/

NINE

Imani Missouri

ROARING DIPLOMAT

This chapter is dedicated to Letha Davis, Anne Darden, my late maternal and paternal grandmothers, and Cashina Jarvis who is alive to witness this moment. When I was seeking clarity and confirmation on being a part of the book, you asked me as I sat on the couch, "What are you over there doing, writing a book?" Unbeknownst to you, that was the confirmation that I needed to be faith and get this done. I love you.

"When you speak, everyone will listen." "You will always stand out amongst the crowd in a positive light." "You will be the next Maxine Waters and Nikki Giovanni!" Those were the words my mother spoke over me and to me as a child. I didn't know the specifics surrounding Aunt Maxine's and Nikki's journey, but I got the gist: they must be powerful women. My mother, Brenda Thompson, a caring, reserved, and rather composed woman would stand tall as she declared these things over my life. I simply looked at her and trusted her conviction. She was and has been consistent with these declarations; ensuring I never forget there is space for my voice and territory for my feet to tread. Whether it be politics and public service like Congresswoman Maxine Waters or writing personal accounts and calls for Black liberation like Nikki Giovanni, God's work within me shall come to pass. His word shall not return to Him void (Isaiah 55:11). I am in full gratitude to my mother, amongst others, for birthing me and cultivating my development so that I can not only hear the possibilities but also see them and use my testimony to draw others higher in their respective journeys.

It is with this context that I pen this chapter on the Who, what, and how in my journey in leadership, specifically calling out injustice in the workplace, advocating for equity, with power, authority, grace, and tact; the latter even in the most tactless and tackiest of situations. In a state of turmoil, how does one maintain their ground? How do you overcome the "fear" of speaking up while exercising self-control? How can you tell if it's the best time for sounding the alarm? If things don't "manifest" the way "you" envisioned, how do you bounce back from the disappointment? While each person's walk is different, there is a unified body for those who believe in Christ. It is my hope and prayer that my reflections and recommendations in these pages will sow a seed of grace-filled activation in your spirit—a diplomatic roar.

When my mother spoke power, light, impact, and influence over me, I was a very shy and quiet child. This may come as a surprise to those who have encountered me in my adulthood. I observed and took notes of my observations, pondered, and either put thoughts on paper or kept them unspoken in an internal secret place. My eldest uncle, a Navy veteran, would quake my mild mannerisms with his baritone and sometimes, brash voice. One day he stood in front of me—towering over me, actually—and said, "Look a person in the eye and let them know you mean business." Elevating his hands, he proceeded to give me a self-defense lesson; my delicate fists in contact with his labor-evident palms. In addition to sharpening my ability to aim and block punches, he reminded me to be alert and communicate "the business" eye to eye. That was a critical turning point in the amplification of my voice. His roar and shield of loving protection over me sparked authority, power, and fight in me. I committed to not letting my uncle down that day. I wanted to prove to him that I would not be silenced. I haven't grown to be nearly as loud as my uncle (I love you, Uncle Jarvis) but that forward, no-nonsense astute nature remains. Truthfully, I am a work in progress.

This past year, the United States has felt the groundswell of fed-upness in the areas of racial injustice. Technology and digital activism provided a medium of exposure to what many communities of color already knew; exposing and unveiling what is deemed as the original sin of this country for those who chose to remain asleep, feigning wokeness. Not only have people taken their frustrations to the streets but they've also shined a light on the racial inequities in the workplace. Additionally, there's a growing reckoning of racial reconciliation in the church. As Laurence Fishbourne yells in Spike Lee's *School Daze*, Waaaaaaaaake uuuuuuuup! (See Ephesians 5:14.)

In this world, and specifically a White-idealistic country (and space), my Blackness is undeniable. There is no phenotypic passing for anything other than Black. I consider it a privilege. Yet this privilege comes with the "ish": perceived threat, expressions that undermine my credibility, and microaggressions couched in naivete. The experiences are very real, the conditions of oppression and accompanying racist behaviors are just downright toxic.

The intersection of race, gender, and faith is quite the trifecta. I have grown to appreciate how God is using me to speak to and model this very intersection. As one of my graduate professors said, "You are so diplomatic." I was offended when this compliment was actually used as critical feedback for how I navigated a tense back and forth with a client. Now, I own it.

When I began my formal journey as a coach, it wasn't Maxwell, Clifton, Tony, or the like who led me (or inspired me for that matter). It was and still is God. I looked for examples of coaches who would represent my experience of the isms in the workplace, and I found a plethora of White men and women and very few Blacks. It seemed like a sea of "follow the leader, leader, leader"; mirroring some hocus pocus witch's brew of a dash of manifestation and financial promotion as the cure to fulfillment. Meanwhile, the roof was on fire! (nod to Soca Boys). That leader wasn't who brought me through and keeps me afloat day to day. I recognize my journey won't speak to everyone, and I am all the way good with that. As a side, you'll encounter colloquialisms in my writing because: one, this is my lovely chapter, and two, it's the authenticity I aim to convey. It will draw those it is meant to draw.

Earlier in my personal walk and professional career, I had a period where I defined myself as more spiritual than Christian. I did this because I was seeking, and I recognized the harm done in religiosity and wanted nothing to do with it. Religion hindered me from seeing God in the day-to-day work. Relationship is what redeemed me. After my maternal grandmother passed away in 2008, less than a month after my college graduation, my faith began to slip. This is part of the reason why I have been called to faith-increasing leaders and organizations. Both have either lost their way in vision or are looking to get re-anchored in purpose. My grandmother was a praying woman. Petite and somewhat unassuming, just like me. It wasn't advisable to cross her. A young White girl in her rural town of South Carolina learned that in the "good trouble" kind of way after spitting on her and calling her the N-word while my grand-mother was a customer at her father's store. My grandmother was one to worship to Mahalia Jackson and Shirley Caesar and also let you know in one way or another "don't come for me unless I send for you". Her fiery faith and wisdom is what I carry with me. I rock her Jesus piece with pride.

When issues of injustice arose in my journey, I remembered my grandmother. I had to practice self-control and move by wisdom even when the fight took a physical, emotional, and spiritual toll on me. When issues prick you, be they personal or professional, it's not always easy to contain your peace. Your emotions may be rocked to the core. Additionally you may experience present-day trauma from things experienced in the past either directly or indirectly as a result of generational trauma. For those who believe in Jesus Christ, this is when you cry out to the Rock (1 Samuel 2:2; Luke 19:40).

Here are eight lessons learned and recommendations for confronting the attacks with wisdom and tact. Please note that this is not all-encompassing, but it will lay a great foundation for your next encounter and further the practicality of faith in action.

1. Determine If This Is Your Fight. I posted a quote in my office—"Don't engage in every battle. If a battle is not between you and your destiny, it's simply a distraction"—as a visual pulse check for me. Every situation does not call for your response. The triggers may evoke an urge to react, but ask yourself: Is this my fight? For me, some of these tests came in passive aggressive emails that could have very well been a phone call or in-person conversation. You know the ones that are sent back to back with a flurry of requests after you left or signed off for the day. Yes, those.
Scripture(s) to Chew On: Deuteronomy 3:22 & Romans 12:19

2. Know What You Are up Against. Isms, while systematically and behaviorally carried out by human agents, are not always visible. Consider overt versus covert racism. The person or institution may very well be a medium for that evil. There is a spiritual component. While there is so much more that can be expanded upon regarding spiritual warfare, know that the fight isn't carnal. Don't let the enemy catch you slippin' because, trust, that is the intent.
Scripture(s) to Chew On: Ephesians 6:10–20 & 1 Peter 5:8

3. Have a Kingdom Strategy. Every tactical force has a strategy. Those gearing up for war seek advice from wise counsel (Luke 14:31–32). I am still growing in this area regarding the "who" for advice and "what" in terms of strategy. I am certain it will be ever-evolving for you as well. God blesses those who diligently seek Him (Hebrews 11:6). Why would this be any different? Your "enemy" doesn't have to know your counsel. Moses refused to move forward without God's presence when leading the Israelites from Sinai to the promised land (Exodus 33:15). I don't know about you, but I would rather have God's presence with me every step of the way, saving me the consequences of impulsive reactions.

Scripture(s) to Chew On: Exodus 33:14–16 & Esther 4

4. Honor Those Who Came Before You. There's a SOLO
YOLO, self-righteous culture running amuck. Proud and ill-
informed people seek the glory for "making boss moves." Let me
burst that self-absorbed bubble. Humility is a vital part of being a
leader. While it's very much possible that you may have a critique of
the status quo (it might not tickle your fancy), the truth is people
have been in the "fight" before you. I have personally referenced
reports, my immediate network, and books when making sound
decisions. You should do the same.
Scripture(s) to Chew On: John 4:38

5. Keep Calm and…. I struggled with impatience for years. The
conundrum is that *I am faith*, which infers patience when the process
and outcome isn't clear. God has been working on me because it has
been quite the challenge. The waiting game for change can feel like
eternity. We have been accustomed to getting things on demand—a
quick fix. Throw justice in the mix and you can hear the flurry of
chants: "We want it NOW!" "No justice, no peace!" On the
contrary, you'll need to take hold of peace so you can move with a
clear head. As my dear friend Angie says, "suck it up, buttercup."
The change is not swift. Be patient and monitor progress, even your
own growth.
Scripture(s) to Chew On: Psalm 46

6. Laugh….God Surely Is. One of my favorite scriptures is
Psalm 37. I remember consuming it for a whole year and a half. I
was working with a heavily toxic supervisor whose goal was to get
her way by any means necessary. If that meant sharing pleasantries
with colleagues she spoke badly about to earn favor, she did it. She
brought in her latest baked "goodies" as bait for conversation. Side-
note: I come from a Black/West Indian family where eating people's
food is a no-no. It doesn't matter how good it smells or how good it
looks. The motives of the cook are not always good (as was the case
with this supervisor), and indulging in the food is like coming into

agreement with their schemes. Now back to this laughter recommendation. I had been privy to unfavorable comments she made about colleagues, including comments about one of my colleague's Christian beliefs. To witness the pretentious performance she carried out on a daily basis irked me to no end. The performative laughter was a test for me. I wanted to bring light to her dark deeds. This called for poise and self-control on my behalf. And you know what, God always gets the last laugh. The Amplified Bible reads Psalm 37 as "The Security of Those Who Trust in the Lord, and the Insecurity of the Wicked." Yvonne Orji, in her book *Bamboozled by Jesus: How God Tricked Me into the Life of My Dreams*, further affirms them in her book by saying, "Whenever you tap into whose you are, someone is bound to be mad that you dared to do what they couldn't, but you can't be responsible for their insecurities and shortcomings" *drops mic*.
Scripture(s) to Chew On: Psalm 37 & Proverbs 23:1–3

7. Praise in Advance of the Victory. In the Old Testament, God's people didn't have the name of Jesus to use as their defense. Praise was (and is) a powerful defense and weapon for deliverance. Remember, your battles are mostly spiritual (Ephesians 6:10–20), contrary to how it might feel in your body. King Jehosophat received a report that opposing armies were coming against Judah. He was alarmed and a little shaken, as any of us would be. His battle plan included seeking God's guidance and proclaiming a fast for the country. The people prayed and fasted, and God gave them battle instructions (2 Chronicles 20:16–17). Get this, the frontline was the praise team (2 Chronicles 20:22). They were singing and praising God in advance of the victory. God caused the opposing armies to fight amongst themselves. Your battle may be working in a toxic department, fighting to prove yourself "worthy" of a promotion, or being undermined for your contributions, slowly eroding your confidence. Whatever it may be, turn up your praise. This may seem illogical, but I know firsthand that when you submit to God's way, the victory will surely follow. I personally had a Disney playlist on repeat to keep me composed. One of my coworkers would even say,

"Disney, Disney" when she saw me getting close to a raging bull. Internally, I was "tryin' not to lose my head," like Grandmaster Flash and The Furious Five. I am human, and as my cousin says I almost "blew my witness" and forgot I wasn't of the world (John 15:19). As simple as it may sound, music and praise helped me shift my posture from one of a pouncing lion to a wise serpent (Matthew 10:6). I have included a playlist to help you in your faith walk. Enjoy!

Scripture(s) to Chew On: 2 Chronicles 20 & Acts 16:25–26

8. Throw Those Hands. You read that correctly, but I don't mean it in the Ludacris "Throw Them Bows" or Crime Mob "Knuck If You Buck" kind of way although sometimes the "trying it" is real. I am talking about Marvin Sapp's "Teach My Hands To War" (Psalm 144:1) kind of way. Because we are being diplomatic and faith-driven here, the hands you're throwing are coming together in a prayer position. 1 Thessalonians 1:16–18 (ESV) reminds us, "Rejoice always, pray without ceasing, give thanks in all circumstances; for this is the will of God in Christ Jesus for you." Trust me that when you're formidable in prayer, you'll be able to stare that opposition in the eye.

Some people are feeling the angst to get on with life and put 2020 behind us. That is: (1) shortsighted (pun intended); and (2) a lack of wisdom. Unless you've been in full seclusion for the past year and a half, it is obvious this country has issues. It would behoove you to not be reflective on the work of God blessing in the midst of this mess. For those who are on the brunt end of injustice, that is not always clear. That is why God has blessed me with Faith Forward LLC.

There are the niceties of God that tend to be the default posture: God is love. This is very much true, but when things in life don't feel as loving, what then? What about those moments when your faith tends to be holding on like a thread because you're hard pressed on every side (2 Corinthians 4:8–12)? Are you able to see God in your work as well as in the four walls of a church? The tests aren't relegated to one sector or area if you haven't realized yet.

I roar for those grappling with similar questions. I roar for God's Kingdom, showing up as best as I can as I am perfected in my faith walk. I roar because of Jesus, the Lion of Judah. I roar diplomatically because God Who leads me is a God of love *and* justice.

Battles are training camps to help you face the Goliaths in your life. Further echoing Yvonne Orji, "When you realize that you're not fighting from the strength of your muscles, but from the strength of your faith, it tips the scales of winning in your favor." With God and His army on my side, "Let me just say this, I'm a strong Black woman and I cannot be intimidated. I cannot be undermined. I cannot be thought to be afraid" (Congresswoman Maxine Waters, March 29, 2017). What's the posture of your roar?

About the Author

IMANI MISSOURI

Imani Missouri is the principal owner of Faith Forward LLC, where she leverages the essence of faith to coach and consult faith-increasing leaders toward their purpose. She also owns a number of faith-centered sub-brands that motivate women of color to reach their full potential in the professional sphere and beyond, including the *Forward 40 (4tea)* podcast, which highlights the experiences of 40 women of color on the rise in the nonprofit and social enterprise sectors.

Imani is also the founder of The Forward Academy, a faith-centered professional development platform for women of color seeking to define themselves beyond their titles. Her career spans leadership roles in the nonprofit, community development, and education sectors.

Imani has been trained and certified as a Personal Development and Executive Coach recognized by the Coaching and Positive Psychology (CaPP) Institute™. She is also an Associate Certified Coach (ACC) with the International Coaching Federation with degrees in Urban Policy Analysis and Management (MS) from The New School and Psychology (BA) from Smith College. She currently serves on the Board of Directors for DIFFvelopment, a nonprofit that creates historically and globally conscious Black visionary leaders who believe in Black business, take responsibility for developing solutions to the issues Black people face, and have unshakable pride and confidence in themselves. She also is a member of the Medal and Nominating Committees for Smith College.

Imani currently resides in the Bronx, the place of her upbringing. She is an avid reader who loves bright colors, soca music, and traveling, especially parts of the world with a rich African diasporic history and culture.

Instagram: @coach_faithforward
LinkedIn: https://www.linkedin.com/in/imani-missouri-27381560
Website: https://www.coachfaithforward.com/
Podcast: https://www.forward4tea.com/forward4tea-podcast
The Forward Academy: https://www.theforwardacademy.com/
DIFFvelopment: https://www.diffvelopment.org/
Roaring Diplomat Apple Playlist: https://music.apple.com/us/playlist/roaring-diplomat/pl.u-oZyl3qeFRKpNE0
Roaring Diplomat Spotify Playlist: https://open.spotify.com/playlist/2XqCBfhNPaWt6RNpLxD8hb?si=fVy6JxMXQzemg-JAhdqXGQ&dl_branch=1&nd=1

TEN

Patricia Pedhom Nono

USING SPIRITUAL FAITH AS A COMPASS FOR LEADING RIGHT

The man to whom much is given, will have to give much; if much is given into his care, of him more will be requested. (Luke 12:48)

In 2004, a young and ambitious lady was landing in New York, ready to conquer the world. Securing a professional internship in New York was a dream come true. I knew nothing about the professional world, but I was eager to learn. There I was in a new city, on a new continent, working a new job, and speaking a new language. I learned from my studies that a decent amount of intelligence and a good dose of hard work was enough to succeed in getting a degree, so it should be the same at work, right?

I was enthusiastic, putting in long hours and ensuring that tasks given to me were completed beyond perfection. Little did I know that the corporate playing field is very different from the graduate school playing field. Twelve months later an intern who started at the same time as I did, Stephan, had been promoted from intern to analyst and from analyst to senior analyst, whereas I was confirmed only at the analyst position. What was Stephan doing better?

After a long weekend of introspection and prayer, I got a strong conviction to ask Stephan directly for the ingredients to his winning recipe. Stephan said he would only tell me over a friendly dinner. He chose a five-star restaurant that was beyond my dining budget. A four-hundred-dollar dinner? Wow! *Well*, I thought, *good advice is priceless*. Now, having moved from that internship to the executive committee arena wherein I managed a team of five hundred, I can say that meal was money well spent.

In this chapter I will share what I learned over dinner with Stephan, all of which was never taught to me in school. I will also share the spiritual habits that help me succeed and what I consider to be the underlying X-Factor to all of Stephan's advice. In doing so, I hope you can avoid the pitfalls I fell into when starting my career as a professional and then as a leader.

Lesson 1: Hard Work Is Required, but It's Not Enough

Working hard is what will allow you to provide quality work, but relationships are what will get you noticed. I worked hard with good results, but I was not networking enough. My colleagues didn't know what I was working on or what great results I was having, and I didn't know what they were up to. Stephan never lost an opportunity to get downstairs with our project manager for an informal chat over a cup of coffee. This helped him get noticed and stay informed on upcoming projects so that he was prepared to work on those high-visibility projects.

Lesson 2: Being Smart Is Good, but Good Exposure Is Better

We often think that our competency and skills are what matters the most. However, even the brightest lamp put under a blanket won't be able to light up the room. Are you able to work on strategic projects that will give you the opportunity to shine, or are you working hard behind the scenes where few people will ever see the good work you are doing? To achieve proper exposure, I realized, it was necessary to have the support of a good leader or manager.

Only a great leader would ensure that your light was able to shine at the right place and at the right time. After talking with Stephan, I understood that I could benefit from being on some high-visibility projects, but I did not know how to discuss that with my boss. One weekend, after reflection and prayer, I wrote an email to my boss in which I said that I could not shine if I was not given opportunity to do so. I was so scared while pressing "send," and, actually, my boss never directly replied to my message, but he started to look at me differently. He began discussing options for projects with me and putting me on higher-visibility projects.

Lesson 3: Don't Play Office Politics—Remain Authentic and Take Responsibility

The consulting industry is extremely competitive with the main mantra being "up or out." Either you succeed or you are ejected. This usually makes room for a lot of backstabbing and work high-jacking between colleagues. People are willing to lie, gossip, finger-point, and take credit for work they have not done. As a young professional, it can be quite tempting to think that this is the way to climb the ladder. I was fortunate enough to have great leaders at the beginning of my career who made a point of limiting office politics and ensuring a healthy social climate within teams. Glenn, a former boss of mine, used to say, "Everyone deserves to defend himself. We do not talk about people who are not in the room. Let's wait for them to be in so that we can have this conversation again." This approach forced us to own the outcomes of our actions and avoid useless finger-pointing. It also forced us to create healthy synergies and ensure that merit-based culture prevailed.

Of course, it is easier to avoid office politics when that is the tone being set at the top. I have also been in environments in which "office politics" were encouraged by the top management, and I saw how destructive it could be for the organization. Let it be destructive for the organization only, not destructive for you. Tomorrow you could change organizations or even managers; you still need to be able to stand by your values, your convictions, and your opinions.

Life is complex and will sometimes throw challenging situations your way. Sometimes a difficult decision has to be made or an unpopular stance has to be taken. During such moments, it will be very tempting to go by the crowd, by what the majority would do or what would please the majority. This is when being stubborn enough to remain you, to remain authentic, is what will differentiate you. When in doubt, choose to act out of service and out of love.

Lesson 4: Shift from the "Power of I" to the "Power of We"

Early in my career, I was a competitive perfectionist to the point that it was hard for me to delegate to my team. It was more about "Me" at the top of the world. Being promoted to manager of a team of five people was the best humbling experience I ever had. I was now responsible for the performance of the unit; it was no longer about my performance but how about how all of us orchestrated together in order to achieve our goals. My first year was catastrophic. The results were not there, the team was unhappy, and I was even called a "work robot." I was so competitive that I lost sight that I was managing people, not players at the service of my performance. It was one of the first times that I had such a blatant feeling of failure. This forced me to ask myself the difficult questions: What is my role now as a leader? What is my role for them? Are they there to serve me or vice versa?

To be honest with you, this was not an easy discussion to have with myself, especially in that it clashed with the common concept of leadership I was taught while growing up. In fact, where I come from, being the leader means being at the top and your team is at your service. The team instinctively works to serve your interests whether you ask for it or not. This was another call for introspection and journey within me. I started documenting myself on organizational performance, on my role as a leader, and on driving high-performing teams. I started also reading my Bible, paying close attention to the kings who impressed me the most: the leadership models of Jesus, King Solomon, and King David. One thing that struck me was that they were servicing, not the reverse. They were servant leaders. They had tremendous successes in managing their kingdoms. (They also had failures, yes, I know, but we can save that for another time.) This forced me to shift the way I saw and lived my values as a leader. Harnessing the "Power of We" became my first priority since being a servant leader. I had to learn to create win–win synergies, plant seeds, and support others.

Winning as a team tastes better than winning on your own. Winning together accelerates organizational performance and the impact on community. It starts by being at service to others, lifting them up, and allowing them to reach the maximum of their potential and therefore increase the potential of the group. Winning as a team is increasingly more difficult to achieve in some organizations because self-interests have taken precedence over group interests. In order to remedy this, we must cultivate and encourage more servant leaders who understand the power of being at service.

Self-Mastery and Spirituality in Servant Leadership

In applying Stephan's advice, I discovered the common thread of lifting up those around you. Supporting others is the X-Factor that makes the rest fall into place. In order to achieve this, I needed to gain self-mastery. Having self-mastery and understanding myself helps me better understand how to respond to my environment and the events happening around me. I have analyzed my mission and the legacy I want to leave, I know the core values and beliefs that define me, and I know the behaviors that help me and the ones that hurt me. All of this introspection is performed with the goal of improving myself so that I can better help and serve others. To me, being a servant leader means being a leader who serves others first. Group interests have precedence over personal interests. Servant leaders seek to lift others and unlock potential in each of their followers. They seek to lead right no matter the adversity. And trust me, leading right is not an easy journey especially when you are in power. Having a compass as reference to keep you on your toes becomes critical. My compass is my spiritual faith.

Developing a personal relationship with God and routines to connect with Him at a deeper level has improved my self-mastery in that it has taught me to listen to my spirit and my body. When something is misaligned with my stars, my inner peace is troubled. This used to be a signal for me that I needed to do some reflection and meditation to connect and listen to God. Now that I have grown up in my faith, I am no longer waiting to have those signals, and I have developed the following habits to ensure I am not taking any decisions without talking to God:

• **Spiritual retreats and self-reflections.** Twice a year or at very important milestones, I usually take a two-day spiritual retreat where I isolate to reflect, pray, read my Bible, and ask for signs in order either to plan my year or to make some difficult decisions. This usually allows me to have more clarity in my decisions. The best innovative ideas I get regarding my career originate from these retreats.

• **Bible readings and meditations.** I connect with God through my Bible readings and meditations at the beginning of the day. I identify passages that resonate the most with me that morning and then meditate on their meaning and how I can apply them to my life. Reading my Bible frequently has allowed me to better anchor the spiritual values and virtues I seek to embody.

• **Prayer.** Prayer for me is a way to connect with God and listen for answers. It is a continuous conversation that is not always formal. I use the following to articulate my formal prayer time:

P – Praise the Lord and thank Him for all the graces, blessings, and trials in your life.
R – Repent for your sins and the sins of others.
A – Ask God for your needs and the needs of others.
Y – Yield and surrender to God's will. Listen to how you feel and what comes up in your mind. And most importantly, take actions on strong convictions you have received.

Having a strong spiritual practice and lifting others are two key components to my success, and I am thankful for people like Stephan and the great leaders I was fortunate to work with, who help me along the way by supporting me and coaching me when I need it. As my way of giving back what I so generously received, my hope for the future is to create the next generation of servant leaders who will serve our communities and dare to lead right. Having more servant leaders in organizations, communities, educations, government, and so on will create many powerful synergies and impacts in the world. As I launch the LeadTitude Academy, my dream is to train one million young servant leaders in three years who will impact their communities and organizations.

About the Author

PATRICIA PEDHOM NONO

Patricia Pedhom Nono is a C-suite executive with a demonstrated record of exceeding profitability goals, turning around under-performing units, and driving increased market share and customer loyalty. She is currently an executive at PwC and lives in Cameroon.

With over 15 years of experience in developing customer-driven growth for companies in Africa and US, she specializes in leading transformation programs with a core focus on customer experience, commercial performance, business optimization, digital transformation and IT management. Entrepreneurial and a creative-thinker at her core, Patricia is at her best when leading the setup of new organizational entities and driving transformation for existing ones.

Patricia views herself as a stubborn servant leader who is also passionate about women & youth economic empowerment and in order to show the next generation that everything is possible for the ones who dare to dream and work hard. "Keep Dreaming" is one of her core values.

LinkedIn:
https://www.linkedin.com/in/patricia-pedhom-nono/

ELEVEN

Nathanael Garrett Novosel

DO WHAT YOU LOVE; LOVE WHAT YOU DO

If I had to summarize what the X-Factor is to success in your career and in life, I could do it with one simple word: Care. If you care about what you do, the people you do it for, and what you get out of the experience, you will find whatever it is deep inside that you need to find to move you forward through anything. Find reasons to care, and you'll have found that X-Factor to go out and crush your career and your life. I can't say that I ever had the most talent or skill in my field, but I knew that I could "out-care" anyone, and that's one of the key ingredients that has made me successful.

So, how does one learn to care more about what they do, and how am I qualified to give guidance on this topic? Well, to answer the latter, I have a unique qualification: I am a high-functioning individual on the Autism Spectrum and have a unique obsession with understanding human behavior both to cover up my social inadequacies and to understand how the world works as effectively as possible. I've studied psychology and related fields for decades, and I've written a book, *The Meaning of Life: A guide to finding your life's purpose*, on the universal drivers of humans' sense of meaning and purpose in life. While I know plenty about the psychology behind learning to care, this chapter is actually going to convey the experiential learnings from my personal journey over my seventeen-year (and counting) career providing research and advisory to the world's leading executives.

The Need to Have Passion for What You Do

When I was graduating from college, I had no idea what I wanted to do for a career. Making matters worse, I had discovered coming into my final year of school that I actually had enough credits to graduate a semester early, meaning I suddenly had to find a job in January when most interviews in the fall were for jobs starting the following summer. Uh-oh. I was graduating with a degree in finance and minors in management information systems and psychology just to show how smart I was in many different subject areas (I called it the "trifecta" of understanding money, technology, and people). All I knew was that I wanted to earn a lot of money and was willing to work hard to do it, but without a clear career objective tied to my major, I had no luck in interviews. I soon found myself out of college with no job and no idea what I could possibly do with my life.

After almost two months of applying for jobs to no avail, I received an out-of-nowhere call from a recruiter at the Corporate Executive Board. The running joke about this company at the time was that, being headquartered in Washington, DC, it sounded like a front for the CIA. They did research for senior executives at large companies; it was an interesting business model of interviewing dozens and dozens of companies until you found someone who solved the biggest challenge that everyone else was facing and profiled the secrets to their success. It sounded absolutely amazing, and with no other options, I felt unbelievably lucky to have a shot at researching the world's best organizations.

However, those insightful profiles are just what the more senior researchers did. I was simply being interviewed for a position as a "short-answer" researcher, meaning that I was a glorified Google searcher looking through the periodical search engine sites like

LexisNexis and Factiva for information on client questions and then sending them the research with a summary of the findings.

It was at this point in my career—that is, not very long into it—where I came to a sudden realization as to how one judges their career. Yes, I had already worked for years as a dishwasher and a dietary aide in high school to earn money for my family and for college. However, the meaning in those jobs was strictly to earn money for food and my future; whether I enjoyed doing the work was less important to me at the time because they were a means to an end. In this thought-intensive white-collar job that could be the start of a forty-five-year career, however, I needed to understand how I was going to keep my motivation to do a job for that long.

My problem was that I still had no idea what I wanted to do with my life. There were things I loved about my job—mainly the vast improvement in getting to exercise my intellect and do new things every day—but there were things that were uninteresting, annoying, suboptimal, anxiety-inducing, and even dreadful. Not knowing what I wanted, how was I supposed to judge whether what I was doing was right for me?

That's when a flash of insight popped into my head: "If you can't do what you love, then love what you do." When I had the revelation that I could learn to love what I was doing so that I could enjoy the journey *and* learn about what I loved to do so that I could (continuously) adjust and improve my destination, I had everything I needed to know about how to assess my career path. For the rest of this chapter, I'll impart as much knowledge as I can to you about how I lived with enthusiasm and purpose in my career and how you can adopt similar principles in your life to (hopefully) do the same.

Love What You Do

We're going to walk through the saying backward because that's both how I leveraged it and also how you're probably going to have to adopt it. I'm a pragmatist and am very risk-averse, so I'm not going to tell you, "Once you find what you enjoy doing, drop everything and go after it!" If you feel the push to do that and you aren't at risk of losing your home or your family, then that could be the approach for you. But I'm going to assume that, whatever you determine that you want to do, you'll likely have to make a smoother transition than that if you can't handle too much stress at once.

You probably noticed that the original saying I came up with had the words, "*If you can't* do what you love" in them, yet the chapter only contains "Do what you love" instead. You see, I didn't know what I wanted to do, so I had no idea how to go after it. Even if I did know, I knew that any path I went on would involve a couple of years of experience in the job I currently had and some savings for the future. If you're reading this, you might be in a similar situation: you either don't know what you want to do or know what you want to do long-term but see the immediate future as biding your time while you gain the money, experience, and skills necessary to move toward that outcome. So that's why we're going to start by talking about how to "love what you do" first.

So, how do you learn to love what you do? Well, this was my first insight in that research position: there will be things in your job that you like and things that you don't like, and there are ways to maximize what you do like and minimize what you don't. Let's cover three critical techniques:

1. Do more of what you like and less of what you don't like.
2. Focus more on what you like and less on what you don't like.
3. Learn to like what you otherwise don't like.

The first one is pretty straightforward: if you have a job where you like some things and don't like others, there are ways to manage your time and effort so you minimize the effect that negative things have on you. One option is to organize your schedule to limit the time and effort you invest in undesirable activities. If you don't like checking email, for example, then incurring the productivity costs of work interruptions by checking your email immediately isn't worth it. Instead, schedule set specific times per day to check it. Another option is that if you work in a team environment, you can see if someone else likes doing a task that you dislike while they dislike another task that you like. If you want to get creative, you can even volunteer to do more of the tasks that you enjoy so that when other tasks require completion, your plate will be too full and your manager will give them to someone else! Combined, these approaches allow you to reduce the burden of undesirable work and increase the amount of desirable work.

In the second approach to love what you do, you can focus more on what you like and less on what you don't like. One option is to engage yourself more in things that you like and find ways to tune out during things you don't like. For example, if you have to do manual tasks like data entry or shelf organizing, then you can put on some headphones, go into autopilot, and crank those tasks out while you're not really thinking too much about them. If you don't like meetings, you can ask to receive the updates via email so that you can better absorb them and respond to them. Another option is to practice activities that make what you don't like seem less bad. Yes, you could hate those thirty minutes where you have to listen to someone's complaints, but the misery from that part of your day or job will be extended if you then complain about that part of your job to five other people for hours afterward. Instead, try taking a few deep breaths and letting the frustration go more quickly. By focusing more on what you like and less on what you don't like, the tasks might be the same, but they sure feel better (or less worse).

In the third approach, you can learn to like what you otherwise don't like by making it more interesting, meaningful, or rewarding. For example, managers who hate small talk but have a team that likes it can make it an agenda item with a goal of team cohesion so that what used to be viewed as a distraction is now seen as relation-ship-building. Athletes who hate certain exercises can play their favorite songs during them or visualize how much better of a competitor they will be in their sport if they get better at them.

Truly, you can reframe your perception of any task. The following steps can help you to inject interest, meaning, or significance into your work:

• **Find what you enjoy and find fulfilling about the experience of doing your job.** If you like to learn, identify all the areas in your job where you get to learn. If you like meeting new people, focus on the opportunities where you get to network at your job.

• **Think about how important or rewarding the result is.** You might not like to complete that resource forecast, but you'll be happy you did when your manager keeps your work–life balance in check as a result.

• **Remember the greater organizational outcome that you are contributing to.** If you are an HR recruiter at a nonprofit organization, for example, remember that every moment of your day is working toward finding the best people who will make your organization's mission a reality. The whole organization relies on you to make sure it has the people it needs to succeed.

• **Visualize the additional value of what your wage or salary gets you.** Your job does not have to be your #1 life priority. Instead, remember that whatever you're doing, you're doing for your family or a passion project outside of work.

• **Reframe your role as your part in getting everything you want.** In more communal societies historically, everyone had a role to keep the house in order. In modern society, this is your contribution to society's function. Fortunately, you get to choose yours and, if you don't like it, you get to choose another. So think about how you're part of a healthy society and how everyone else is doing work for your benefit just like you are for theirs.

By following these mental reminders, you will maximize your appreciation and enjoyment of what you do and minimize your perception of any negatives that can drain or demotivate you. My favorite example from my early career was that I did the math on how many executives I could help with my research and how many jobs I could save, promotions I could facilitate, and barriers to success I could help them break through with my work. It was millions of dollars' worth and thousands of people's worth of potential impact, and so I felt compelled to do my best work possible.

Do What You Love

So you've done all you can to make what you're currently doing as interesting and rewarding as possible, and you've reached your limit. You know that this isn't ultimately what you want to do, but you don't know what that is. What can you do to find out what you love to do?

Back to my story as an example: it took me many, many years to figure out what I wanted to do. The irony is that I ended up with the greatest luck in history: I was hired into a field that I am both great at and enjoy by pure chance. If you're curious, the way I got the research job was a series of lucky occurrences, from someone named Brooke (to this day, I don't know who Brooke is, but thanks, Brooke!) finding my résumé on an online job site and referring me for the $500 referral bonus to my hiring manager seeing something on that résumé that told him that I would do whatever it took to succeed. So you'd think that this luck (or help from fate/the divine/the universe for the spiritual reading this) would make it hard for me to know how to find what you love, but on the contrary: I didn't know that I was doing something I liked because I didn't know what I was looking for!

So let me use my early career to explain how I figured it out after many years. As I mentioned before, I noticed that there will be things you like and don't like about your job. The goal is not only to define what those are within your job but also to define them in general if you either could pick any job or if you didn't have to work at all. It was only after doing both of those things that I realized that I was already on the right path. Here's how it works:

• **Define what you enjoy doing and what provides value to others.** This was the missing piece for me, but it should go first if it can (it's okay if you don't know and have to come back to it, though). I finally realized that I liked learning and teaching, solving problems, understanding some new idea or insight, delivering it to someone else, and then having that person's life be changed for the better as a result. I literally did all of that in my job and got to have greater and greater impact as I moved up in my career, so I finally realized that I was on the right path. But if you're on the wrong path, you'll need to identify career options that get you doing more of what you like to do, what you're good at, and what provides value to others.

• **Identify what you like/don't like and next steps in your career that will maximize that ratio.** This can be used to make subtle changes or life-changing ones. For example, in my career path, I had to pick between being a researcher or an advisor. I ultimately picked advisory because I loved helping people and giving that perfect explanation of an idea, and I found a way to sneak in some new content creation once in a while so I wouldn't miss it too much. So, your next step could just be deciding between two positions that are similar, and you just have to see which one increases your like/don't like ratio in the near term and long term. If you move into a completely different field, however, that involves a new degree, then you'll have to make sure that the desire for the skills, activities, and income associated with that new role makes it worth it. If you're unsure because you're scared of the unknown, you probably want it; if you're unsure because you're not sure whether you'd like it, take baby steps instead of giant leaps. The only way you'll know whether you like something is if you experience it.

• **Ensure that every step in your career will continue to enhance why you like your job.** As we mentioned, you might like the money, the impact you make, what you actually do, or how you help the organization overall. In any case, make sure the next step for you keeps you moving forward in those areas—not just the money or social status. People talk about the "Peter Principle" (i.e., getting promoted to your point of incompetence) a lot, but people don't talk as much about getting promoted to a position where you lose your passion or interest. Some people aren't meant to be managers; others aren't meant to overspecialize if they like doing many different things. Make sure that your next career step is as much of a net positive as possible and not a trade-off between money/status (i.e., what you think might make you happy) and purpose/enthusiasm for what you do (i.e., what may actually make you happy).

• **Monitor for changes within yourself about what motivates you.** This is the one that people usually don't see coming. You might get everything you thought you wanted and then realize that you didn't want it, or you might get everything you thought you wanted and then realize that you're satisfied and want to do something else now. You might have kids and decide that you want to be a stay-at-home parent, or you might want to start your own company or simply work part-time at something meaningful and reduce your stress levels. Your growth areas are always subject to change, so don't keep moving in the same direction if your better judgment tells you that your priorities have changed.

If you follow the above steps, you can both do what you love *and* love what you do. If you are just starting out, it's okay to find ways to love what you're doing while you figure out what you can do in life that you love. You have many goals in life, so it's perfectly okay to work at a job that earns more money so that you and your family can live the lifestyle you want even if you don't find the job as engaging. It's also okay to take a pay cut and reduce your standard of living so that your life feels more meaningful doing something that is your passion. What matters is that you are living the life you want and feel fulfilled as a result.

So that's how I learned ways to care more about what I did at any given time so that I could put my maximum effort and enthusiasm into it. On a final note, you'll notice that this chapter is written relatively agnostic in a book about spiritual secrets; this is intentional. In my research, I have found that many spiritual and scientific techniques are identical in practice and only differ in terms of whether the person exercising them believes that a nonphysical influence is involved. For example, you can read this chapter and conclude that I am helping you gather the information you need for your intuition to guide you (spirituality) or I am simply helping you logically, rationally think through what matters to you in life (psychology). Either way, the same principles apply:

- You need time to think and process your emotions regarding your career direction.
- You need to appreciate what you have as you continue to strive for more.
- You need to figure out what matters to you and what drives you.
- You need to get the necessary support both to figure this out and to help you move forward.
- You need to follow ethics that help you feel good about what you're doing and how you're doing it.
- You need to make choices every day that keep you growing and thriving.
- You need to look at your life holistically, including your health, wealth, social life, family, knowledge, and contribution to others/society.
- You need to find guidance, meaning, and purpose from within. Only you can accurately determine what success looks like for you.

When you look at the foregoing list, you'll see that regardless of whether you rely more on meditation, spiritual guidance, and signs from the universe/God or logic, reason, and science to figure things out, getting those things right will lead to great outcomes in your career and your life.

Now, get out there and figure out how *you* can best contribute to your own growth goals and to society, and learn to love the journey!

About the Author

NATHANAEL GARRETT NOVOSEL

Nathanael Garrett Novosel is an award-winning researcher and advisor with over twenty years of experience studying individual and group behavior and over fifteen advising the world's leading executives. In 2020, he wrote *The Meaning of Life: A guide to finding your life's purpose*, a book dissecting the eight core concepts underlying all philosophies and religions that have scientific evidence supporting their role in people finding meaning in their lives. The book has won over eleven awards and accolades and been featured on over a dozen podcasts.

Nathanael spent much of his life trying to understand people, life, and meaning after his father abandoned him as a child and he struggled to fit in due to what he would find out later was Autism Spectrum Disorder. After years of using these insights to help the world's leading executives solve their most pressing organizational challenges, he wrote a book summarizing his findings over the years regarding living a life of meaning and purpose. He resides in Myrtle Beach and enjoys writing, nature, warm weather, and anything that reminds him of his hometown of Pittsburgh, Pennsylvania.

My Book: *The Meaning of Life: A guide to finding your life's purpose*
Website: https://www.yourmeaninginlife.com
Twitter and Facebook Handle: @LifetheBook
LinkedIn: https://www.linkedin.com/in/nate-novosel-50436b32/

TWELVE

Patience Ogunbona

ACHIEVING PRESENCE, POSITION, AND PROFIT

We are spiritual beings having a human experience. —Jolene Halas

Spiritual awakening is the pursuit of purpose and meaning in life. From a very young age, I was acutely aware of an ache and dissatisfaction with my life and a strong need to define purpose. I believe that since we are spirit, collaborating with God who is spirit is the key to living a purpose-driven life. No one finds fulfilment until they truly feel they are living a purposeful life.

It wasn't until my early thirties that I discovered I was introverted. But the signs were there; I craved solitude and literally fought hard to disappear and spend time listening to God and immersing myself in absorbing scriptures and feeding my intuition. During these formative years, I developed a hunger for the blessing and empowerment that the following scripture promises:

"God blessed them, and said, be fruitful, multiply, replenish the earth, subdue it and have dominion over the fish of the sea, the fowl of the air, and every living thing that moves upon the earth." (Genesis 1:28)

According to Søren Kierkegaard, "life can only be understood backwards; but it must be lived forwards." The slower pace of life in 2020 (an introvert's dream), gave me space to look back through my life from childhood to working in corporate for over fifteen years as an audit professional to now running my own business as a coach, trainer, and speaker who works with introverted female entrepreneurs and leaders as well as corporations offering tailored training on leadership and team dynamics. I have deciphered three key stages (presence, positioning, and profit) of spiritual awakening I experienced over the years that have defined purposeful living and helped me step up into my leadership potential.

Presence - First Awakening - Fruitfulness, 2013

"Eek! I cannot go out looking like that!" I shrieked as I looked at my reflection in the mirror. My younger sister came running because she knew if she let me have the last word, I would back out and not go through with my makeup appointments. The makeup artist was at a loss. In frustration she said to me, "But, madam, you said you wanted to stand out and be the centre of attention. This is how we do makeup to be bold so you get the effect."

I said to my sister, "I am not sure about being this bold, big eyelashes, orange lips, bright blushing cheeks and gold eyeshadow. This is more makeup than I have ever used in my whole lifetime."

My sister encouraged me by saying, "This is your day. You wanted this, and you need to follow through. You will be proud you did. I know you struggle to love yourself, but believe me, you look stunning."

Indeed I had to follow through, this was an epic moment in my life. I was turning forty and preparing for my "coming out party": the coming out of Patience Ojochide Ogunbona. I was finally going to show up on Earth. I have felt invisible all my life, inconsequential, self-loathing, and small. My sister was right, I had to give myself permission to be loud and proud, something I had withheld from myself for years, feeling like I was living out an identity crisis, never really showing up on Earth, each time wearing a mask of happiness yet knowing there was more that needed to feel right before I could truly be happy.

"Be yourself, everyone else is taken." —Oscar Wilde

So if I wasn't being myself, who am I? After years of searching, it was time to stop hoping someone would finally give me the permission to be me, to shine, to do what lights me up. It was time to answer this question and peel back the layers. I was ready: makeup, flowing outfit, long well-gelled hair, my well-orchestrated party, my speech and musical performance, everything was planned to the very last detail as an announcement. It was time to be PRESENT.

I remember the feeling of standing in a hall of over two hundred people, delivering my speech, singing on stage. My nieces who came from London ran to me saying, "Aunty, we can't believe how great this party is, we showed our mum and she is so proud of you."

It felt really good; many were impressed. That day I performed a song by Crystal Lewis and Ron Kenoly. The song's chorus became an apt anthem in my life for the things I wanted to see about myself to replace the image I had held on to for most of my life. I wanted to feel beautiful, bold, brave, and take action on long-held dreams, to stop feeling crappy and depressed every day. I sang it loud. I was never going back to who I was. After the party, I felt empowered. I didn't just impress others, I impressed myself. I felt proud. It had given me a confidence boost.

Next was my birthday present. I planned something big, too. It was the next stage of my unveiling. I was heading to Las Vegas with my family. I am a rebel at heart and very independent-minded. However, I lived in fear of not being the "good girl" or being seen as fun-loving and carefree. The fear of what people would think of me plagued me and caused me to shrink. I felt that the best way to announce my independent and "naughty" side was to head off to Sin City and finally let everyone know that "I sin too, and I am okay with it."

There was also another reason. I had shrunk so much that I struggled to see my potential, with the increased self-awareness I was getting, being present also meant bigger and better. At the time, I couldn't think about anywhere other than Las Vegas to visualise bigger and better, with its audacious over-the-top expressions, bright lights, hotels, and shows, everything is big and bold.

What about the temptation to gamble, the explicit sexual expressions? I wanted to live in the real world and not feel that I had no self-control or would give in to anything and everything, the real world and not the church was the right place to test my strengths of self-discipline and "good girl qualities." On this trip I was determined to have a real mindset and vision shift, conquer fears, begin to aim higher, and start to lose the fear of people's judgement. I really wanted to start exploring who I was on a deeper level, how big were my aspirations, and what price I was willing to pay to accomplish them. I took along with me *See You at Top* by Zig Ziglar. One of Zig's quotes in the book states: "You don't have to be great to start, but you have to start to be great." Looking back, I realise that by initiating challenges to conquer and grow, I was beginning to take full responsibility for becoming who I wanted to be and truly embracing self-leadership.

"Every challenge introduces a person to himself." —John MacDonnell

Once you feel you have a presence, you can position yourself. Having presence means that I am acknowledged, I matter, and my contribution makes a difference. My character, flawed or perfect, deserved an airing, and I have value to bring to the world and position myself to achieve purpose and profit. It is soul-destroying to feel like you don't matter or belong. I had felt that way for most of my life until then. Through divine relationship and intervention, I find myself leading and living my life with purpose.

My mum said I slept from the moment I was born. I hardly opened my eyes even to eat. By nine years of age, I was desperate to keep sleeping, very aware of being depressed and suppressed by my reality. I slept at least twelve hours a day. Half of it was closing my eyes and daydreaming. I experienced freedom to be my true self and create a world I would love to live in. One day, sitting against the wall in my childhood home, I had my hands locked and placed above my head. I was deep in thought as my dad walked past me. In African tradition, crossing your hands over your head signalled feeling overwhelmed, despondent, and lost.

My dad said to me, "Stop doing that. What are you thinking about?"

To which I replied, "I am thinking about life."

Dad laughed and said, "Life! I feed, clothe, and put a roof over your head. What else is there to be thinking about in despair?"

He had a point, but from this early age, I had the constant nagging question of, "What is the meaning of life and the purpose of my existence?" In my head there had to be more to life, I desired to live with careless abandon and freedom, but, alas, I was a carefree free-dom-seeker in a very controlled world. I couldn't fathom how God wanted me to live in a world like this. There was so much spark and life in me that needed full expression.

So I had this dialogue with God: "When a car is made, it is named by the creator (e.g., Mercedes) and everyone knows who that is and what the car is about. The car also comes with a manual, which states what each component is and what it does. If it needs servic-ing, you take it to the garage where the manual is used to fix it or it goes back to the creators to be fixed. We also know that the reason a Mercedes is created is to be driven and to provide a service to its owner." My 9 year old self was now asking God, "Why did you make me [what is my purpose], and where is my manual to live purposefully?"

To my surprise, God responded: "Stick with me and I will show and tell you your purpose. Keep living each day with intention and courage. Let's work together to bring your daydreams and imaginations to life."

I said, "Okay then, deal! If you will keep telling me pieces of the purpose manual as I go along, I will keep listening and following through."

By my teens, I had gotten into a deeper relationship with God, I read the story of Esau and Jacob from the Bible, and it left an impression on me. Esau was the first-born son, and Jacob was the second-born son and the schemer who connived with his mother and stole the birth right bestowed by fathers upon the first-born child from under Esau's nose. In despair, Esau cried out to God and God said: "You will live by your sword, and you will serve your brother. But when you decide to break free, you will shake his yoke from your neck" (Genesis 27:40).

For some reason, this story struck me. I really felt like Esau, like life had dealt me a tough hand, even though outwardly I had loving parents who in their own way did their best, I still really felt like life was against me. God promised me that I would know when it was time to break free and take this heavy yoke of feeling out of place, despondency, and self-loathing off my neck and be free. With all that I initiated in 2013, I felt that I had truly taken the yoke off and was beginning to experience true freedom to be seen and be more.

These actions ignited passion in me. Now I started to walk and work towards the next phase of my purpose journey: positioning myself to fulfil purpose.

Positioning – Second Awakening – Multiplication, 2014–2020

Although I had begun to feel that life had meaning and purpose, come 2014, I had a sense that there was more to uncover. Back then, I loved being an internal auditor, and I found strength to begin to make progress and climb up the career ladder. I was beginning to know and grow myself. I had discovered that I am introverted and love being me. I now believed that what I desired in life was what I deserved. I was pals with God; my relationship with him was great. This was the calm before the storm.

Mum had been ill for a few years, but it took a turn for the worse. On February 24, 2014, I woke up to the most horrendous message of my life. My dad was on the line at 2:00 a.m.: "Danger! Danger! Your mum is in the mortuary." My life stopped. *This cannot be real.* I went into shock from the trauma, one I did not recover from until 2021.

From then on, life felt like a baptism of fire. Here I am again feeling like a big yoke had been placed on me. I questioned God, "Why didn't you let me save her?" Mum was meant to fly into the United Kingdom to start her treatment on Friday. We were excited. Finally, she was granted a two-year visa. But, alas, it was false hope; she died on Tuesday. From then on, I went into safety mode. I was disappointed. I resented God and the people around me. To protect myself, I resisted the pull for further growth. However, I also started to tentatively explore what to do with my trauma. I didn't want to waste Mum's death. I wanted to build on her legacy. She lived for others and gave her life to serve them. Despite my pain and fears, I felt the pull towards serving others; somehow, divine intervention prevailed.

I had followed John Maxwell for years having read his book *Today Matters.* This helped solidify my self-leadership, making strides each day by living intentionally. I heard that he had a coaching programme. Having explored and obtained a certificate in coaching, I wanted to know more. I spoke to a sales representative. It felt like the next level. Coaching and leadership training would allow me to position myself and carry on Mum's legacy of helping others. But I got scared. Who was I to do this? Broken-hearted from my loss, I felt like all the years of growth was not enough to take a leap. The sales representative understood my pain from death and loss and shared her story. As a five-year cancer survivor, she gave me perspective to see that "The key to truly dealing with fear and pain was to focus on living and growing to my full potential." Mum would want me to do this, so I signed up. But I did nothing more.

By December 2016, bouts of cluster headaches landed me in Accident and Emergency three days in a row. On the fourth day, I woke up and had lost sight in my left eye; my peripheral vision was gone due to nerve damage from a suspected stroke. It was there, desperate about the direction my life was taking, I spoke to God and promised that if he would give me my sight back, I would commit to following through with growth and serving others. Miraculously, I got my sight back and then began the journey to create a coaching, speaking, and training business that has taken me around the world serving in the United Kingdom, Nigeria, the United States, Asia, the United Arab Emirates, online and live.

By the end of 2017. After another tragedy where I lost my brother-in-law, I was again heartbroken. I was struggling to pursue multiplication of my potential whilst working. I took a huge leap of faith and left my job. In 2018, I started my business fully and ran a few signature workshops, wrote and self-published my first book, *Aspiration to Transformation (10 Steps to Get You From a Place of Discomfort to Your Empowerment Zone)*, created my first three-month coaching programme, and started to make progress and get results. From the end of 2018 to the end of 2019, I was in another battle for my life; ill health plagued me and my immunity was at an all-time low. I felt very alone too. In the midst of this battle and disappointment with God, again I cried out in prayer, and He said, "You will be fine," and "I shall give you the gift of strangers."

When we think of buried potential, we expect to discover it accidentally perhaps without much pain and effort. But, like precious metal, we go through God's "refiner's fire" to deliver precious beauty and potential from beneath the surface.

> "I will refine them like silver and test them like gold. They will call on my name, and I will answer them. I will say, 'They are my people,' and they will say, 'The LORD is our God'." (Zecharia 13:9)

Holding on to God's promise, I walked into 2020 feeling very frustrated with this fire. I decided to seek out his help and use the gift of solitude and a slower pace of life brought on by the pandemic to go on a ninety-day awakening journey. My keyword for 2020 was Connection. I hired a coach and revisited my nine-year-old self. This led to a rebirth as The Visionary Introverted Woman, positioning myself to serve other introverted women who wanted to be successful entrepreneurs and leaders. The "refiner's fire" is when God uses the challenges of life like fire to refine us to be co-creators with him. When refined, we see the strengths in us to triumph, live a purposeful life, and be a blessing to others. With God's refinement, my challenges with identity, self-acceptance, and embracing my uniqueness have become the foundations upon which I have come to embrace introversion as my identity and allow it to give my life purpose and meaning as well as multiply my happiness by serving others.

Profit - Third Awakening - Replenishment, 2021 - Beyond

"The best way to find yourself is to lose yourself in the service of others." —Mahatma Gandhi

Refinement is like growing pains, which are of no value if there is no change and increase. Lessons learnt are meant to bring an increase in the quality of your life, the people you meet, and the outcomes you create for yourself and others. By 2021, I had been on the John Maxwell Team for almost five years. I never saw myself as a leader until the "refiner's fire" awakened a desire in me to lead a tribe of other introverted women who are yet to find their own breakthrough in life and business, helping them to take off their masks, shine from the "refiner's fire," embrace their introversion, and leverage their growth pains and strengths to thrive in an extroverted world. According to Seth Godin:

"Tribes are about faith, the belief in an idea, and in a community of like-minded people. Many people are beginning to realise that working on stuff they believe in is much more satisfying than just getting a paycheck. Consumers have decided to spend time and money on brands because of their stories, things that matter to them and what they believe in."

Leadership is about identifying a tribe you can serve with excellence. This is when you begin to profit. I could never have predicted how my journey would detour to wanting to lead a tribe, but as William Shakespeare says: "The meaning of life is to find your gift, the purpose of life is to give it away." Profit is much more than money; it is fulfilment, happiness, and satisfaction derived from serving others. I mentioned that in 2019, God had said that he would give me the gift of strangers, well! Towards the end of 2020, I wanted to develop my leadership skills to be worthy of leading a tribe. I signed up for a sixteen-week Ultimate Leadership Programme with Keith Ferrazi, which led to setting "moonshot goals." A moonshot goal is a goal that is so big that you cannot accomplish it on your own.

My moonshot goal is to reach and help at least two thousand introverted women by the end of 2021. This goal led me to create a successful summit for female introverted entrepreneurs in August 2021, where I collaborated with twenty-seven other speakers. This book is part of my moonshot goal. I leave you with this promise I lean on:

"For I know the plans I have for you," declares the Lord, "plans to prosper you and not to harm you, plans to give you a hope and a future." (Jeremiah 29:11)

About the Author

PATIENCE OGUNBONA

Patience Ogunbona is a corporate and business trainer, aligned business strategist, certified transformational coach, inspirational speaker, DISC personality expert, emotional intelligence expert, and the author of a personal development book titled *Aspiration to Transformation: 10 Simple Steps to Move You from a Place of Discomfort to Your Empowerment Zone.*

Patience is the founder of Aspire-Transform-Inspire (ATI-Coaching, Consulting & Training Ltd), a CPD-accredited coaching and training company that offers tailored world class resources, services, training, and speaking to help organisations add value to their staff and ensure strategic alignment to their mission, vision, and objectives. Helping them achieve sustainability and profitability by training on leadership, inclusion, diversity, employee engagement, and emotional intelligence.

Patience is also known as "The Visionary Introverted Woman" passionate about empowering introverted female entrepreneurs and professionals to overcome self-doubt and develop high performance business strategies and leadership skills to create increased presence and position themselves in their marketplace to attract consistent leads, clients, income, and profit.

Patience has been a quarter and semi-finalist in the John Maxwell Stagetime speaking competition, and has spoken on stages and facilitated bespoke training and roundtable discussions in Orlando, Las

Vegas, the UK, Nigeria, and Costa Rica. She runs her own weekly live show called *Inspiration to Achieve*. Her motto is: "Impossible is an opinion, feel free to disagree and carve your own path and journey to success". She looks forward to being part of your transformational journey and success.

Facebook: www.facebook.com/ati-coaching1
Instagram: www.intsagram.com/patienceogunbona1
LinkedIn: www.linkedin.com/in/patience-ogunbona
Websites:
www.patienceogunbona.com
www.ati-coaching.com

THIRTEEN

J. Scott Scherer

FROM THE OPEN HEARTH TO THE BONSAI: A PATH TO DEEPER MEANING AT WORK

What you fear will not go away: it will take you into yourself and bless you and keep you. That's the world, and we all live there.

—William Stafford, *For My Young Friends Who Are Afraid*

The Open Hearth Encounter

"You're early. Why don't you step inside?" His white beard shimmered with the orange glow of the open hearth behind me. I turned to peer into a cave of fire two stories tall, a roaring industrial furnace where raw metal elements melt under extreme heat to produce molten steel. The sweet, sour odor of iron laced my nostrils, like the smell of sweat. Men in hard hats carrying lunch buckets waded toward their lockers.

The gnome-like foreman waved me into his 10' x 10' glassed-in office with a blank wooden desk, a beige metal filing cabinet, and two thinly padded black vinyl chairs. Through the tinted glass I saw the open hearth spitting fire. The 7:00 a.m. shift started soon. I lowered myself into a chair.

Less than a year ago, in the spring of 1981, U.S. Steel's executive training program recruited me as an economics major right out of Duke University, one of ten candidates harvested in a nationwide search, slated someday to populate the C-suite of this macho mega-corporation. My first six months I spent in the Philadelphia sales office. Some days I wondered if I'd made the right choice. My heart felt dead at times. I wondered if I fit in here. I was afraid of what it would mean if I didn't. But the job paid well, and I had loans to repay.

My training on the mill floor started at Fairless Works, a sprawling, city-sized steel manufacturing complex twenty miles north of Philadelphia. I'd traded my preppy blue blazer and wing-tip shoes for a full-body heat suit and steel-toed boots. I felt on edge and was trying not to show it. Would the mill workers try to toughen up this know-it-all college kid from the management program? Yet the foreman in front of me seemed congenial, his voice padded by his snow-white beard. My shoulders eased.

Our conversation unfolded. About ten minutes in he paused and shifted in his chair. I can still feel the gaze of his blue-gray eyes, the hot glow of the open hearth flashing through the glass onto his plump cheeks.

"You remind me of a young man I once knew whose life was completely upended one night by a dream he had." He nodded as he studied me.

My larynx knotted. *How could he possibly know about my dream? I hadn't told anyone. That was seven years ago. I'd been running from it ever since.*

The foreman carried on. "Shaken by his dream, the young man wandered over to his parish priest's house in the middle of the night and knocked on the door. The priest opened the door saying, 'Where have you been, I've been waiting for you?' He invited him in and handed him a copy, *The Dark Night of the Soul,* a sixteenth-century spiritual classic by John of the Cross." At which point my bearded foreman slowly pulled open the top drawer of his wooden desk and pulled out a fading, typed-out version of the first chapter of *The Dark Night.* "Here, I think this is meant for you." I reached out to take the pages, unable to grasp what just happened.

I didn't remember much of my twenty-mile freeway drive home that night. I parked my red Honda Civic hatchback on the street then waded into the living room of our Society Hill brownstone with its scuffed hardwood floors. My roommates were both upstairs. Sitting on the secondhand sofa in front of the fireplace, I looked down at the typed pages in my hands and filled with gratitude. Three months later, my training was done. U.S. Steel transferred me to St. Louis for my first job placement. Despite ranking at the top of my class, I resigned before completing my first month. The day before I resigned, I had called up Fr. John Wall, an entrepreneurial priest I met in passing while on a retreat my last semester at Duke. I did not attempt to hide the confusion in my voice. I felt lost. I needed to figure out my life's direction. I didn't know where I belonged, but I knew I didn't belong in St. Louis. I asked him if he could help. He created a volunteer position for me on the spot. I wouldn't get paid, but he'd house and feed me. I felt saved.

Back in Philly, I loaded up my U-Haul trailer and headed off to the retreat center in North Carolina, which would be my base. I did not realize it till decades later, but I was following the path of the man in the story as prescribed by the gnome in the mill. I knocked on the priest's door. I was invited in. My soul was asking: "Where have you been? I've been waiting for you."

Soul Quest: A Pilgrim's Path

Nestled in the Carolina pines, far from the fast-track Fortune 20 world, I felt free from the squeeze of the achievement vice. The volunteer gig I'd signed up for seemed doable: raise some money to support youth retreat programs. Compared to an executive track program, this church life left plenty of space to explore my inner world. For a life-long overachiever, this felt like parole, just me and my soul. This was our getaway time. A big reader, I dove headfirst into books, studying the inner life in all its dimensions.

I had a head start. Before I left Philly, I had written to Dr. M. Scott Peck, author of *The Road Less Traveled*. A classic work, it encouraged the reader on the path of deep self-exploration. I told Peck of a foreboding angst that seemed to trail me and asked him for advice. His warm, hand-signed letter guided me on a path to psychotherapy. Peck's taking time to write a personal letter to a random reader like me felt like a needed arm around my shoulder.

I read greedily of the lives of historic figures who'd mined the inner world, people like Carl Jung and Thomas Merton. Jung's autobiography, *Memories, Dreams, Reflections*, explored the world of dreams and imagination. His brave forays into the depths of the psyche exposed me to the immensity of our inner world and the primacy of dreams, which spoke to me and gave me solace. Merton's autobiography, *The Seven Story Mountain*, struck me. Just out of Columbia University, Merton left behind a promising academic and writing career, opting instead to live out the rest of his days in a Trappist monastery in the foothills of Kentucky. Merton's bold departure from his expected professional path encouraged me.

But I was not drawn to monastic life; that would not suit me. I loved business. The business world was my home turf, my baseball diamond, my gridiron, my center court. I did not want to give it up. I just wanted to find a way to do business with more meaning. As the months rolled on, I managed to juggle my fundraising work with my soul spelunking. I took a grant writing course, started applying to philanthropic foundations. We started raising some money. Meanwhile, I continued my reading binge, diving into centuries-old writings by mystics and monastics and poets. I wanted to learn from those who'd gone before me on this path. With mounds of wise tomes surrounding me, my soul came off the respirator. I was not earning a dime, but I felt alive.

One night back at the office, Fr. Wall, my boss who was fast becoming a friend, sat me down and asked if I would be interested in putting together a pilgrimage as a way to cultivate relationships with our donors.

"What's a pilgrimage?" I asked.

"I'll show you," he said.

Less than a year later, Fr. Wall and I were strolling at dusk through the medieval streets of Assisi, where the beloved St. Francis of Assisi, a twelfth-century mystic, lived his holy and joyfully iconoclastic life. We had forty eager pilgrims in tow. I strolled past the illuminated Basilica of St. Francis and returned to my room in the nearby Windsor Savoia Hotel. I fell back in exhaustion onto my thin mattress. I recalled earlier that day how an elderly lady in our group began to weep as she traced her fingers along the rock walls of Francis's hermitage cave, still thick with his humble spirit and how our pilgrims were gripped by the story of Francis who, eight hundred years earlier, had stood on the very same town square and, stripping naked, delivered his audacious "No!" to his father's acquisitive lifestyle.

Something was happening inside these people. What was it? We were in a place far away from home, remote enough to make them feel a bit disoriented, a sacred place soaked in archetypal stories. Most people came with an open-hearted intention, some with secret wounds. We walked and talked and prayed and ate and drank and laughed together. Such simple activities, yet I felt something moving inside me. Beneath the cobblestones of our personas, an alchemy was at work. Like the open hearth back at U.S. Steel, with its mix of primordial elements, pilgrimage seemed to pack its own transformative heat. Lying on that bare bed, arms spread, staring up at the wood-beamed ceiling, I felt at once a bone-deep exhaustion and a heart penetrating sense of purpose. Unknown to me, pilgrimage was working its magic, and I was being groomed to serve in its court.

Once I'd finished my volunteer fundraising tenure, I started organizing overseas pilgrimage groups out of my two-bedroom apartment in a red brick quadruplex in Raleigh. I felt drawn to pilgrimage. Pilgrimage, I'd discovered, was really an outer journey to an inner place. While on pilgrimage, people accessed a deeper place inside themselves, and once home, they began to live from that deeper place. To be a midwife to this transformational process called to me. Plenty of missteps followed in birthing the business. Work was slow to come. Then the first Gulf War hit in late 1990. Overnight, international travel froze, and all my trips were cancelled. I was cooked and completely broke. Not just broke. I was in debt to the tune of over $27,000, distributed ecumenically across nine different credit cards. I felt crushed. Dire. I looked around and wondered aloud to God: "What are you up to here?"

One day, not that long after, grace extended a generous hand in the most unexpected way. On my first ever trip to the West Coast, I got introduced unexpectedly to a veteran in the religious group travel business, Henry Avakian, a savvy Egyptian-Armenian gent in his late fifties. Henry had retired early from travel but got bored and wanted back in the ring. He wanted to start a Catholic pilgrimage company. Imagine! Henry had the means. He needed a younger partner. He'd be the equity; I'd be the sweat. Would I move to Los Angeles? Of course. Besides, I was broke. Two months later, days after my thirty-second birthday, I was back in a U-Haul, driving three thousand lonely miles to a state of thirty million inhabitants where I knew only two people. It was 1991 when we launched our company, Catholic Travel Centre: Worldwide Tours & Pilgrimages, offering spiritual journeys to fifteen countries on three continents. For three short years I sat at Henry's feet daily, garnering lessons from his twenty-plus years in the pilgrimage trade, grateful for his wisdom. Our brand-new company blossomed. On October 23, 1994, my mentor and now dear friend went in for heart bypass surgery. His last words, heading out the door to the hospital, as he slapped me on the back, were: "It's your ship now. Sail it!" Three days later, Henry was gone.

Birth of the Bonsai Business Model

That autumn I woke up each morning in shock at the loss of my colleague and lunch buddy, treading in a tsunami of responsibility. Overnight, at age thirty-five, I became the sole owner, manager, and financier of an international pilgrimage business. Yet, I felt a twinge of excitement. Up to this point, I'd experienced two formative work cultures: the corporate business world at U.S. Steel and the soul world of the Roman Catholic Church, each of which left me wanting. Now, situated in the liminal space between the business world and the soul world, I had the chance to combine elements of each.

Our company flourished as we refined our systems. Once we achieved $10 million in annual revenue, peers in the industry urged us to grow bigger. "Scale it!" But something in me resisted. I'd begun to adopt an old Latin phrase as our company motto: *non multa, sed multem*. "Not many, but much." We had enough. I assured my colleagues we were growing all the time, just not in size. We grew in quality. We grew in intimacy with our suppliers and our customers. While bigger meant more money, I feared a social diseconomy of scale would erode the intimacy of our relationships. After some years at the ship's helm, I felt the need for more camaraderie with business peers. Being a business owner can feel lonely, and I did. Plus, I wanted to mature my business management skills. Spurred by my soulful studies in the pines of Carolina, I wondered where to go to study business management with a social conscience.

One spring morning while doing my ab crunches on the bedroom floor of my Los Angeles condo and listening to National Public Radio, I heard an advertisement for the Peter F. Drucker Graduate School of Management. Long considered the Father of Modern Management, Drucker was my hero. He broke onto the management scene with his encyclopedic tome, *The Practice of Management*. What drew me to Drucker was his strong sense of social responsibility, which aligned with my perspective. A month later, I enrolled in the Drucker School's Executive Management Program.

In the winter of 2006, the Drucker School invited Charles Handy, noted writer and longtime host of a BBC Sunday radio program, to guest-teach a course with his wife, Liz. I jumped at the chance. Born in Ireland, the son of a pastor, educated at Oxford, and with an MBA from MIT's Sloan School, Handy had co-founded the London School of Business. He reflected deeply about business and society and had written many reflective books, including the international bestseller, *The Age of Paradox*. Charles asked us to make a class presentation in a course he called *The Still Life*, where you reflected on your life's direction through the medium of a personal "Still Life" composition of significant objects from your world. One of my objects, among others, was a bonsai. During my class presentation, I introduced my inside-out business philosophy, which I called the Bonsai Business Model (BBM), using the metaphor of a bonsai to show how leading a business was akin to raising a bonsai —business as a living art form that brought beauty to the world through vision and creativity, heartful care, a sense of harmony, close relationship, and the practice of right proportions. I'd been formulating the tenets of the BBM over a couple years as I mated my years of inner exploration with my emergent role as a business owner. The class offered an opportunity to share the model for the first time. As I spoke, I noticed Handy sitting in the back of the room, nodding.

That evening Charles appeared as a guest on National Public Radio's *Marketplace* program with Kai Ryssdal. Ryssdal and Handy were old radio pals, and Kai often invited Charles onto the popular business news program when Charles was in the States. On air, Handy talked that evening about the BBM, a novel approach to business he'd learned about earlier that day from one of the executives at the Drucker School. Charles encouraged me to write about the BBM, so I launched a website, BonsaiBusinessModel.com. Over the next decade, I continued my in-depth inner work, but in a more business-oriented idiom. The emerging field of professional coaching was asking deeper questions about the workplace, so I jumped at the opportunity to get certified. Some coaching schools, such as San Francisco-based New Ventures West (NVW), founded by coaching pioneer James Flaherty, adopted an integrated, developmental approach, one which drew me to its door. NVW's Integral Coaching™ model considers all dimensions of the person— somatic, relational, emotional, cognitive and spiritual.

I credit NVW with driving home to me the primary role of practice as a path to growth and lasting change. I grew up in the Catholic world where the emphasis was weighted toward ortho*doxy*, less ortho*praxy*—an emphasis on knowing versus experiencing. While my reading of the monastics introduced me to the importance of spiritual practice, it was NVW and their coaching methods that opened my eyes to the central role of experience, moving beyond mere understanding. I began to seek out practices, like breathwork and gratitude practice. Mindfulness meditation surfaced as an option, but I found myself more drawn to its cousin, the practice of contemplative prayer, specifically a daily practice called Centering Prayer. Benedictine monk Fr. Thomas Keating popularized this contemplative practice. Contemplative prayer brings the mind into the heart and yields a letting go into God. This receptive method slowed me down, taught me to surrender.

About the same time as I took to Centering Prayer, I explored another practice that has since become a mainstay for me. The practice is called Focusing, pioneered by Eugene Gendlin in the 1950s. Gendlin, a PhD candidate in philosophy at the University of Chicago, was gifted with Jedi powers of observation. In his work with pioneering therapist Carl Rogers, Gendlin noticed how certain people during therapy experienced a felt shift. He hypothesized that perhaps something about the way these people processed their internal experience determined whether they would achieve the change they sought. He outlined their internal process in a method he called Focusing, coining along way the now-popular term "felt sense."

Numerous disciples of Gendlin's formed tributaries off his original work. The school of Focusing I follow is called Inner Relationship Focusing, led by the brilliant Barbara McGavin and Ann Weiser Cornell. Ann's book, *Focusing in Clinical Practice: The Essence of Change*, is still the single best handbook I've encountered on how to achieve lasting change. For me, Focusing became a regular practice, teaching me how to relate to my internal experience and articulate the seemingly inarticulable, how to turn toward and be with what I most feared, to enable me to live more freely and more fully. Combined with Centering Prayer, these two practices became my rudder and my sail. Meanwhile, over the years, our pilgrimage company continued to strengthen. Our client base stood at 95 percent repeat and referred business. We'd become a leader in our industry. We had served more than thirty-five thousand pilgrims. The year 2020, leading up to our thirtieth anniversary in 2021, promised to be our strongest ever.

But COVID-19 had different plans for us in 2020.

COVID-19 news broke big late in February that year while I was traveling in the Holy Land with a high-profile client, a noted New York Times bestselling author, along with one hundred of his organization's friends and benefactors. By then only a handful of COVID-19 cases had surfaced in the United States, notably in Seattle. Two nights into the pilgrimage, my phone rang in the car on my way out to dinner with the group's tour guides. On the line was the assistant to the celebrity leader.

"Scott, I need you to come back here, now."

"Sure. Why?" I didn't like something in his voice.

"You know the COVID case in Seattle that's all over the news?"

"Yes, of course."

"Well, the doctor who treated that young man in the Seattle emergency room...she's on our trip!"

After nail-biting phone calls to the Israel Ministry of Health and the Ministry of Tourism, we were able to continue the pilgrimage as planned, though the emergency room doctor needed to quarantine. Once I got back home, though, the dark dominos of COVID-19 began to fall in unsettling succession. We faced urgent challenges on multiple fronts: operations, accounting, and public relations. In operations, we had groups caught overseas who had to be rerouted and flown home prior to their scheduled return, before international airports shut down. Airlines were writing and rewriting their policies on the fly. Who had a pandemic policy? The hotel industry was no better equipped. The Italian parliament decided to protect their hoteliers and so passed emergency legislation permitting hotels to retain deposits that had been refundable under the original contract. So, our money was locked up. Some overseas hotels shut down and did not answer our entreaties for weeks. With seventy-five group departures on the books, our ops department had to unwind hundreds of reservations—airlines, hotels, restaurants, buses, guides.

Over a course of five turbulent months, our accounting department pressed hard to refund thousands of pilgrims while trying to extract our own refunds from overseas suppliers. Registrants started demanding immediate refunds. Calls started coming into the Better Business Bureau. Customers were panicking. Meantime, California issued a work-from-home order, so our team had to conduct this entire fire drill from our kitchen tables. Overnight we launched a communications campaign to tighten our connection with our customers. Still, I winced when I opened my email inbox. Each day felt like crossing a field of sniper fire. Most people were gracious and patient, a small vocal minority made life heavy and sleep a luxury. When my family asked how I was doing, I told them I felt like I was shoveling a driveway full of snow with a teaspoon.

In time, as months rolled on, we managed the mountain of cancellations and refunds, writing off tens of thousands of dollars in non-recoverable expenses. Our team made an Olympian effort. I leaned heavily on my practices: Focusing, which enabled me to turn toward what I feared, and Centering Prayer, holding me in its loving embrace as I surrendered hour by hour to the unknown. On the interpersonal level, what carried our team through our dark nights at sea were the close relationships with our key clients, namely, the leaders of the organizations who'd entrusted us to manage their group's travel. Those leaders buoyed us with their ongoing presence and nurturing support. Thanks to our motto, "Not many, but much," the rooted, heartful relationships we'd cultivated over the many years kept us standing. In the end, our BBM withstood the nuclear stress test.

My Odyssey Continues

I began telling this story at the mighty open hearth, and I bring it to a close, here, with the diminutive and mighty bonsai. I traced a thirty-year odyssey, my continued attempt to bring meaning and work into harmony in the world of business. Along the way I shared resources that guided me: dreamwork, psychology, coaching, poetry, pilgrimage, Focusing, and prayer. And I shared a model I developed, the BBM, which serves as a compass, guiding me in how I lead my own niche business. Throughout this telling, I tried to call attention to the role of the soul in work, and how to make room for it, whatever one's work may be.

James Hillman, founder of a movement called archetypal psychology, refers to the soul as "that unknown component which makes meaning possible, turns events into experiences, [and] is communicated in love." The L-word sneaks in there, one we are not often comfortable to include in the workplace. Maybe we should invite it in and find a way for it to stay. I see what I had wanted all along was for my work to become a way for me to love the world.

About the Author

J. SCOTT SCHERER

A chance encounter in his early twenties with a daimon-like foreman in a steel mill steered Scott off the executive suite track of a Fortune 20 company and on to a pilgrim's path, ultimately founding one of the country's preeminent boutique religious travel companies, which recently celebrated its thirty-year anniversary. Scott's counter-cultural, inside-out approach to business, which he calls *The Bonsai Business Model*, provides a compass for entrepreneurs seeking to grow an enterprise based on meaning and beauty rather than sheer size.

Educated in economics at Duke University, Scott continued his master's studies at the Peter F. Drucker and Masatoshi Ito Graduate School of Management, the namesake of one of his management heroes, Peter Drucker. The son of a Pennsylvania State Hall of Fame football coach, Scott was groomed on disciplined practice as a path to excellence. Ultimately, he pursued his own coaching career but of a different ilk, receiving his certification in Integral Coaching™ from San Francisco-based New Ventures West, under the leadership of coaching pioneer James Flaherty.

Scott resides in Pasadena, California, where he manages his pilgrimage travel company and maintains his executive and life-coaching practice. An avid writer and poet with a contemplative bent, his writing challenges entrepreneurs and executives to pursue a deeper path of self-discovery and revelation.

FOURTEEN

Sukanya Lahiri Soderland

INSIGHTS FOR 21ST CENTURY LEADERS FROM THE
WISDOM WELL OF THE AGES

I was born into a rich spiritual tradition with a guru, Paramahansa Yogananda, founder of Self- Realization Fellowship, and a path that honors the underlying harmony of all true religions. I tend to keep my spiritual life private; it is something so special that it cannot be expressed fully. Moreover, I'm mindful of the risk of unwittingly diminishing or desecrating something so sacred amidst the glare of public spotlights. Yet, something in me stirred when I saw the title of this book, compelling me to share reflections that have proven helpful in my ongoing pursuit of peace, success, and contentment.

I have had two realizations through my professional life—one at a system-wide level, another at an individual leadership level—that are prompting me to share more about the spiritual side within. First, much of my career motivation to date has been trying to catalyze transformation in health care through innovation; promoting better health and well-being for others and a movement toward greater proactive, preventative health care that allows people to live better. What has become increasingly clear to me both personally and professionally is that better health care is partly predicated on finding ways to motivate people to make healthy choices preemptively.[1] I believe that one way to help people make healthy choices is to help them tap into and enhance their own sense of well-being. We know that an interconnected web of lifestyle factors are a major cause of chronic disease and also affect mental health. These include how people manage stress, what they eat, how much they exercise, how much they sleep, how connected they feel to others, and whether they feel a sense of purpose in their life. Once people get sick, modern medicine can work wonders, and pills and procedures are vital in today's system. However, to arrest health problems before they fully emerge, more is needed. One of the fundamental needs for a large-scale preventative health care approach is to help people tap into their own inner strength, power, and potential and get along with themselves and others better.

The second realization I have had in my years working as a management consultant and senior executive in large organizations is that leadership matters, and the nature of leadership required moving forward is changing significantly. Given the frenetic rate of change we see across industries and society, the one changeless constant seems to be that we are living in a world of "VUCA" or volatility, uncertainty, complexity, and ambiguity. I believe that many of the qualities required to drive large-scale transformational leadership in organizations now are distinctly different from prior decades' conceptions of leadership strengths. And these strengths increasingly draw away from traditional ego-led command and control approaches toward a more uniquely soul-led way of igniting the limitless potential of others, inspiring progress toward a higher purpose, and being secure in one's own strength and self-worth.

It is with this backdrop and humility that I share a selection of learnings from my attempts to apply the wisdom of the ages in my life. They are lessons I continue to learn, stumble over, and relearn over the years.

The Inner Work Enriches the Outer Work and Brings Balance

The Bible states, "Seek first the kingdom of God and his right-eousness, and all these things shall be added unto you."[2] However, I have had periods of my life where I told myself I was "too busy" to do more than the minimal spiritual and self-care routines that are part of my daily discipline. What I've found over the years is that while there may be periods of "go-go-go" push and long hours, I'm at my best when I make the time to tune in to the inner work. For me this includes twice daily prayer, yoga meditation, and deep breathing. Multiple times a week it also includes self-care rituals with potential health benefits: "forest-bathing"[3] with my family, prac-ticing gratitude,[4] and writing in my journal.[5] There can be real pleasure in soaking in the simple joys of appreciating a beautiful sunset in the sky, leaves waving at you in the breeze, or being greeted by a cheerful smile from a stranger.

When I've skated by, doing the bare minimum inner work for multiple days in a row, I find that I feel off-kilter, like something is just not right. My poise becomes ruffled, and my mind is more rest-less. By contrast, when I'm making the time and the effort around the inner work, the outer work (professional or even at home) feels effortless. Fresh creativity abounds, my objectivity increases, my effi-ciency multiplies, my intuition sharpens, my sense of connectivity to and compassion for others grows, and there is a spirit of deep unflappable calm. Meditation has become easier over the years, and it is now no wonder to me that scientists demonstrate a growing bevy of its benefits from better concentration and psychological well-being[6] to improvements in health conditions such as high blood pressure.[7]

I've come to realize that making the time and commitment to the inner work enriches the outer work I do—in terms of both quality of productivity and my relationships with others. Whereas before I'd do my basic practices and no more unless there was ample time, I now make time for the inner work first. While there can be bumps along the way, I do this secure in knowing that my investment in well-being will produce greater benefits and yield all-round balance in life.

Finding this sense of balance has often been a challenge for me as a working professional, wife, mom, and daughter. Beyond my spiritual practice, I've historically put family and work above all other pursuits, sometimes putting in seventy-. eighty-, and even hundred-hour weeks to do my very best on the work and home fronts. This has often come at the expense of sleep, daily exercise, and taking care of mundane practicalities such as car inspections and passport renewals.

I got a wake-up call on this front several years ago when my daughter was very young and we were preparing for her maiden voyage to my ancestral land, India, to visit with our extended family. Soon after Christmas, my daughter and I were snuggling up reading a book on a Saturday evening when my husband poked his head in and matter-of-factly said, "Your visa for India is expired." He can be a bit of a jokester, so I just laughed him off and kept reading. He insisted that I look and, lo, not only was my visa expired, but my passport was as well! Our flight for India left the next day. In five days, my parents were hosting a big formal party for our daughter in Kolkata. What ensued was a spectacular whirlwind of events that illustrated to me that it was much simpler to keep on top of all aspects of life versus excelling in a few areas while neglecting others.

My husband and daughter left the next day with my parents from Boston for India. I entrained for New York in the hopes of finagling both an updated passport and an emergency visa during a holiday week with limited office hours and virtually no remaining tickets to fly to India in time for the big event. With great faith, determined affirmations, and God's grace, I managed to receive the coveted visa and passport in New York a mere few hours before I was to board a flight from Boston to India. The whole episode was intense, and as I finally let out a sigh of relief as I boarded the flight, I reflected on the learnings from this extraordinary experience. In Hinduism there is a saying that doing any one duty at the expense of others (e.g., work at the expense of health) is not actually properly fulfilling the duty at all. This event was a great turning point for me to much more conscientiously seek balance in life.

Do Your Best, Let Go of the Rest

My motto has long been "do your best, let go of the rest." My goal each day is to do my best and strive for excellence. This has often come with external rewards and achievements. However, I've learned (and continue to learn) that it is quite liberating to separate doing my best from any expectation of external recognition or validation, especially since so much is not in our control. One of my most striking realizations of this truth came years ago on my birthday.

I was preparing to pick my daughter up from gymnastics class and was lost in thought on how to redecorate the art in our stairwell. The next thing I knew, I was emerging from what seemed like a deep sleep, slowly recognizing that I had fallen head-first on the ice on my driveway. After struggling to get up, I carried on with my day, but after a week of headaches and not feeling well, I realized that I'd suffered a concussion. I began my short-term disability leave with every determination that I'd be back in the office in no time. My husband initially even had to hide my phone to ensure that I would stay off my work email. I had been accustomed to working hard and putting my mind to anything and getting it done, no matter whether it required staying up all odd hours of the night and running on long-spent adrenaline.

Yet this time was different. I learned that the doctors predicted that I would not be able to return to my rigorous role as a partner at a management consulting firm, flying to different clients in multiple cities each week and working long hours. And then fear set in. Fear of not being able to pay our monthly mortgage bills, fear of leaving a job with a role that I quite enjoyed, fear of not being able to use my brain in ways I took for granted. It wasn't until I decided to let go of the fear, to truly "let go and let God," that the healing came rushing forth, allowing me to make a full recovery.

As I returned to work after three months of leave, I made a set of determinations for what I'd do differently moving forward, ranging from the mundane (no more than two cups of tea a day) to the more significant (no more worrying about work items outside of my control). To that end, I resolved that as a relatively new partner in consulting, I would no longer worry for a moment as to whether I'd meet my annual multi-million-dollar sales targets. I would continue to be sincere in doing my utmost with enthusiasm but would let go of predicting or perseverating over the results. That resolution held and worked like a charm.

There are, of course, times when what I had hoped for does not manifest as desired. With full faith, I receive what comes as what I need for my lifelong personal growth. I may not comprehend why until years after, or perhaps ever, but there is a great serenity that unfolds with that acceptance.

I find this truth to do your best without looking for the fruits of those actions, expounded upon in depth in the *Bhagavad Gita*,[8] to be enormously powerful. The mental freedom it offers helps reduce stress and yields benefits from an overall mental, emotional, and physical health standpoint. And yet I also find it to be quite difficult to fully maintain amidst the battles of daily activity. It can feel like a tightrope walk: balancing against the ego's gravitational pull to either get sufficient external validation or pull back, and the soul's desire to shine brightly, secure in its inner validation and faith.

As You Sow, so You Reap

The world's great scriptures each espouse the importance of moral living. The Bible's "whatever one sows, that will he also reap" precept[9], the Ten Commandments, and the *Bhagavad Gita*'s exposition on the importance of karma and living rightly (the moral code of the yamas and niyamas) are deeply ingrained in how I aim to live my life. Service is perhaps one of the greatest examples of seeing the law of karma in action: most of us can relate to how personally rewarding it can feel ("helper's high") to actively help someone else in a meaningful way. These positive feelings from helping others appear to be affirmed as health benefits according to research.[10]

What I've discovered is that the trust one engenders by living with high integrity, character, and consistency is deeply powerful and is felt by most people. In the consulting world, a big part of the role of a consulting partner is to serve as the "trusted advisor" to senior executives. Some of the biggest trust-building moments arose when I told a senior client that he did not need to purchase a big expensive project to achieve his objective, even when he knew that my own compensation was dependent on selling such projects.

What I'm working on now is elevating beyond the basic "do's and don'ts" to a higher level of challenges that recognize that thoughts are a force.[11] As such, I'm aiming to be extra careful with my thoughts and activity. I know that how I focus my attention and what I think and see will impact who I am and how I am with others. I've introspected that at times when I feel I need to relax because I'm tired and want an escape, some of what I characterize to myself as "relaxing" me-time is not truly relaxing. To that end, I've had periods of mindless "doom scrolling" before elections, reading up on every article of news, with fewer hours of sleep as the result. I now try to be more discerning about where to invest my time reading in detail versus simply scanning headlines to stay abreast of current affairs. I now often move my phone into grayscale mode to turn off the extra dopamine hits from the bright colors and spend my free time recharging with more creative pursuits such as singing. A good friend of mine goes further and declares one weekend day each week as digital detox, citing emerging studies that highlight the potential benefits to sleep, connectedness, mental health, and overall well-being.[12].

This all seems well and good when all is well, but how does it work with people we may find difficult to get along with? What I've found to work well with challenging clients in the past has been genuinely seeking out their most endearing qualities and immediately mentally recalling those positive qualities whenever difficulty with them arises. When they've held a view that I find to defy my own logic, I've become curious about what it is about who they are and how they view themselves and the world that makes them think that way. This approach has been enormously helpful in enabling me to be sincere and authentic with them, to learn more about where they are coming from, and has proven productive in substantially improving the situation.

That said, I have been in situations where the circumstances have been particularly trying. I have grown to understand that difficulties with others are often mirrors for self-introspection. Sometimes people with whom we have the most difficulty serve as a trigger to see what it is about what they value, represent, or bring out in ourselves that we don't like or have yet to work on ourselves. When someone says or does something that is not in keeping with what I view as just, I am careful about what role I play in response. After feeling and processing the human emotions involved and then taking the "balcony view" of the situation to uncover learnings, it is usually not worth thinking too much more about. That said, there is always the need for discriminative wisdom and situational fluency as I've also been taught to have courage, while also wishing others well. Sincerely wishing others well can be remarkable; studies suggest it has a positive impact on personal well-being by reducing stress and anxiety, improving empathy and happiness, and improving one's sense of connectedness.[13] In the *Bhagavad Gita*, Krishna says to Arjuna, "O Arjuna, the best type of yogi is he who feels for others, whether in grief or in pleasure, even as he feels for himself" (Yogananda, p. 637). Full forgiveness, unstinting compassion, and gratitude for the opportunity for self-growth is liberating and can help release the energy we keep tied up in knots when someone is bothering us, allowing us to move forward in our lives with freedom and inner self-confidence.

We Each Have Infinite Potential with Our Own Unique Soul-Led Trademarks

Jesus said, "The kingdom of God is within you."[14] I believe we each have limitless potential in our souls, and each bears its own special trademark characteristics that no one else can fully replicate. Yet our soul's light is often covered up with layers of gunk: ego-driven needs, trauma-born pain, unregulated emotions, and so on. As we peel off those layers by getting our ego out of the way, our soul takes on the leading role and our soul's light, our own unique potential, brightens and expands. As Paramahansa Yogananda, known as the pioneering father of yoga in the West, wrote, "You realize that all along there was something tremendous within you, and you did not know it." With this realization anchored in, there is no scope for the ego to creep in with doubt and insecurity about one's own self-worth. With inner security and a cool calm confidence, we are not looking for external validation by trying to prove how good we are or to get ahead by cutting others down or to pretend we are someone that we are not. Instead, we are motivated and empowered to serve, inspire, and help others. We embody a "growth mindset"[15] of abundance where the proverbial pie expands and there is room for all versus a "fixed mindset" of scarcity where there is a shrinking pie and a need to elbow others out of the way to maintain our own share. We are constantly looking for opportunities for self-improvement and ways to learn from and support others.[16]

In this modern era, we have more opportunities to be our authentic selves and express our uniqueness without having to force fit into preconceived molds of what successful leadership looks like. In my consulting days, I was often the only female and only person of color in the room, with a name that many found hard to pronounce and a young-looking face. We were counseled by some tenured team members to take on the interests of our clients (e.g., become an avid sports enthusiast) in order to connect with them. I knew that would not be authentic for me as I had little interest in sports, save for watching certain live games. I took the path less traveled and have since counseled many others to do the same. Being authentic, a kind smile, taking an interest in others and getting to know people on a deeper level can go a long way and even win over those with whom we may seemingly have little in common. As the first non-white female partner at the global management consultancy where I worked, my personal style was different from many in the leadership ranks. Times have shifted, however, and there is far more widespread awareness of the diverse ways in which one can be highly effective without fitting the traditional leadership archetype. As a parent and leader, I am particularly keen to embody and cultivate this orientation. We are each unique in what we offer and the role we play in this world. Think of how much personal drama, organizational challenges, and societal strife could be reduced with a wider spread appreciation of these truths!

Superpowers for 21st Century Leaders

In the age of the 2020s and beyond, the x-factor insights for self-transformation and transformational leadership of organizations draw from the well of the eternal wisdom from the world's great traditions. These insights can be considered as superpowers as they can be accessed by each of us to aid in realizing our higher potential and leading others. These superpowers include:

• an ability to manage and enhance one's own energy and wellspring of well-being and to inspire others to do the same;

• an abiding inner confidence that stems from a true understanding of our own uniquely magnificent inner potential that does not rely on external validation for support;

• emotional regulation and the ability to keep calm and maintain objectivity while understanding the perspective of others with empathy and compassion;

• trust in ourselves and the ability to engender others' trust through consistently high integrity behavior;

• a curious growth-oriented mindset that flourishes with opportunities to learn and to promote others to succeed;

• a finely tuned intellect, fresh creativity, and a wisdom-born intuition that can adapt with ease while remaining true to oneself; and

• a clear sense of purpose that governs the individual and organizations to achieve a greater good by helping others.

These superpowers are super for a reason—they are hard to achieve and maintain and yet can yield extraordinary results, starting with improved all-around health and well-being for the individual. Each of these superpowers represents a journey, and some days are easier for us to be our best selves than others. Some of the lessons we need to learn in this school of life come back to us if not learned or become harder as we graduate to more advanced classes. However, with deep self-compassion and self-love, knowing we are doing our best, and letting go of the rest, we can "try and try again," with no guilt and no regrets. Over time, we will faithfully reach our goal. As we clear the path by learning the lessons life stores for us, we open new vistas for our soul's potential. "A saint is a sinner who never gave up."

Endnotes

1. Shaffer, Joyce. "Neuroplasticity and Clinical Practice: Building Brain Power for Health." *Frontiers in Psychology*, vol. 7, 2016, doi:10.3389/fpsyg.2016.01118.

2. Matthew 6:33, "But seek first the kingdom of God and His righteousness, and all these things will be added unto you." www.biblehub.com/matthew/6-33.htm.

3. Li, Qing. "The Benefits of 'Forest Bathing'." *Time*, Time, 1 May 2018, https://time.com/5259602/japanese-forest-bathing/.

4. "Giving Thanks Can Make You Happier." *Harvard Health*, 14 Aug. 2021, www.health.harvard.edu/healthbeat/giving-thanks-can-make-you-happier.

5. Smyth, Joshua M., et al. "Online Positive Affect Journaling in the

Improvement of Mental Distress and Well-Being in General Medical Patients with Elevated Anxiety Symptoms: A Preliminary Randomized Controlled Trial." *JMIR Mental Health*, vol. 5, no. 4, 2018, doi:10.2196/11290.

6. Walton, Alice G., "7 Ways Meditation Can Actually Change the Brain." *Forbes*, Forbes Magazine, April 2021, www.forbes.com/sites/alicegwalton/2015/02/09/7-ways-meditation-can-actually-change the-brain/?sh=25983b411465.

7. "Meditation: In Depth." *National Center for Complementary and Integrative Health*, U.S. Department of Health and Human Services, www.nccih.nih.gov/health/meditation-in-depth.

8. Yogananda, Paramahansa. *God Talks with Arjuna: The Bhagavad Gita: Royal Science of God-Realization: The Immortal Dialogue between Soul and Spirit: A New Translation and Commentary*. Self-Realization Fellowship, 2001, pp: 1015–1017.

9. Galatians 6:7, "Do not be deceived: God is not to be mocked. Whatever a man sows, that will he also reap." biblehub.com/galatians/6-7.htm.

10. "Helping Others Is Good for Your Health", *Psychology Today*. 4 Sept., 2020, www.psychologytoday.com/us/blog/insights-more-meaningful-existence/202009/helping-others-is-good-your health.

11. University, Stanford. "How the Human Mind Shapes Reality." *Stanford News*, 13 June 2018, https://news.stanford.edu/2018/06/11/four-ways-human-mind-shapes-reality/.

12. Radtke, Theda, and Apel, Theresa. "Digital Detox: An Effective Solution in the Smartphone Era? A Systematic Literature Review - Theda Radtke, Theresa APEL, KONSTANTIN Schenkel, Jan KELLER, Eike Von Lindern, 2021." *SAGE Journals*, journals.sagepub.com/doi/full/10.1177/20501579211028647.

13. "Wishing Others Well May Boost Your Own Well-Being." *Medical News Today*, MediLexicon International, www.medicalnewstoday.com/articles/324843.

14. Luke 17:21, "Nor will they say, 'See here!' or 'See there!' For indeed, the kingdom of God is within you.", biblehub.com/luke/17-21.htm.

15. Dweck, Carol S., *Mindset: The New Psychology of Success*. Ballantine Books, 2016.

16. Ibid.

About the Author

SUKANYA LAHIRI SODERLAND

Sukanya Lahiri Soderland has spent the last two decades as a consultant and strategist to the business world.

Recognized as a national thought leader in healthcare, Sukanya speaks often on a cause she is passionate about: catalyzing large-scale systemic change in healthcare through innovation. Sukanya served as a senior Partner at Oliver Wyman, a global management consulting firm, where she consulted to large healthcare companies and co-founded the Oliver Wyman Health Innovation Center. Currently she serves on the executive leadership team of Blue Cross Blue Shield of Massachusetts, where she holds the role of Senior Vice President of Strategy, Innovation, Consulting and Enterprise Data & Analytics. She graduated *magna cum laude* from Harvard College and received her MBA from the Harvard Business School.

A recipient of the Working Mother Top 100 Award, she continually strives to find ways to maintain balance in her family and work life. She is a Founding Member of Chief and sits on the Advisory Board of The Trustees of Reservations. She is motivated by personal growth and helping others recognize and realize their fuller potential as transformational leaders.

In Sukanya's chapter, she illuminates insights from her lifelong spiritual foundation. She is deeply committed to the inward journey of alignment to her purpose and views her spiritual life as the anchor for all that she does.

LinkedIn:
https://www.linkedin.com/in/sukanya-soderland/

FIFTEEN

Christina Thomas

ARE YOU LISTENING?

The Dream

I was walking in a heavily crowded area. There were people talking on all sides of me, and it was incredibly loud. My heart started to beat faster and faster and my breath became shallower. I tried to walk straight, but people kept bumping into me. I felt them on my left and right. Nothing about where I was seemed familiar, so I started to get scared. My eyes were open, but I couldn't see. Everything was completely dark, and then I realized I was blindfolded. When I noticed that, I began to panic. Every time I tried to walk by myself, I would trip over something or run into somebody. I had no idea who was around me, and although others were trying to guide me, I didn't trust them.

Then, I heard my husband's voice. Although it was loud and there were other people speaking to me, his voice cut through the noise like a sharp knife. The moment I heard his voice, my anxiety began to be relieved. He guided me to him, and I followed every direction to a tee. I desperately wanted to find him because he was my safe place and only way out. Even when I made it close to him, I couldn't help but try to get as near to him as possible. The closer I was, the more comfort I felt and the clearer I could hear him. So, I clung to him and I listened to every word.

That was the dream that woke me up…literally and figuratively. You see, the night before, I was on my knees saying the only words that I could seem to utter, "Why aren't you answering me?" I was angry, I was hurt, and that was all I had to say to God. I felt like everything was crashing down around me, and I desperately needed answers. I couldn't help but wonder, out of all times, why God would abandon me now. This was when I needed Him the most but no matter how much I called out, all I received was silence. Questions began to race through my head: "Did I do something wrong?"; "Did God leave me?"; "Is He angry with me?"; "Am I praying wrong?"; "Can He not hear me?" No matter how many questions raced through my head, I couldn't answer them. I started to get frustrated because more questions began to circle in my mind, and I felt myself going to a place that I didn't know how to get myself out of; so, I decided to go to sleep.

After the dream, I began to question whether all this time God wasn't talking or whether I just wasn't listening. I couldn't shake the feeling that I had the dream for a reason. So, I began to analyze it. I replayed everything that happened and questioned what my dream was telling me. One of the things that came to my mind was how I was able to hear my husband's voice over everyone else's.

What came to me was one word: relationship.

That was it! That was the key. I wasn't able to hear God's voice because I wasn't sure what it sounded like, and further than that, I wasn't taking the time to listen. In the dream, I was able to discern the voice of my husband because I knew his voice. My husband and I have spoken to each other and spent enough time together for me to be able to distinguish his voice from that of anyone else's. However, I couldn't say the same when it came to my relationship with God.

In a relationship, there is usually a courting phase that occurs before the relationship forms a bond. I remember when I was dating my husband, we would talk all the time. And when I say "all the time," I mean it. We would spend hours on the phone (sometimes even falling asleep on the phone), we would share stories about our day, we would check in with each other throughout the day, and when we weren't with each other, please believe, we were thinking about each other. We enjoyed being around each other, and no matter how busy we were, we always made time for one another. Our relationship was a priority.

Does that sound like your relationship with God?

If it doesn't, don't feel bad. I am not asking this question to condemn, shame, or judge you; I am asking this question to make you think.

When I asked myself this question, I wasn't able to answer in the affirmative. My time with God consisted of waking up, reading a verse or two or a devotional, praying, and then, boom, I was off to start my day. The only time that I thought about God during the day was if something bad happened or I was praying over my food. It sounds bad as I am writing this, but it's the truth. I just didn't have the time (so I thought) to devote to going "deep" with God. I felt like the time that I spent was enough.

I was raised in the church, and what was emphasized, I did. I was spending time first thing in the morning reading and praying. So, I didn't understand why, if I was doing what I was supposed to be doing, I wasn't getting the results I wanted to get.

What I didn't realize was that our relationship remained at a surface level because I invested surface-like time.

My time with God became just another part of my to-do list. Once I checked the box, I didn't feel the need to revisit it; it was done for the day.

It took me a while to understand that it is less about quantity than it is about quality. You see, you can spend all day with God, just as a couple can spend all day together, but if that time isn't of quality, the relationship isn't going to progress, at least not in the manner that you would desire. I don't believe God is concerned about the amount of time that we spend with Him, but what I do believe He is concerned with is how we spend the time and our hearts when we spend time with Him.

My time with God often got derailed because I would receive a text, scroll on Instagram, think about what needed to be done that day, and so on. I was more concerned with the time I was spending rather than the way I was spending that time. My motive wasn't to grow closer to God and get to know Him on an intimate level; it was to do what people said I should do.

Another issue I noticed was that during my time with God, I was the only one speaking. As I said, I was focused on reading and praying. During the entire time with God, my mind was either focused on reading or my mouth was moving. This was true even after my time with God ended. I never slowed down during my day to clear my mind, be quiet, and listen.

Imagine you were in a relationship where only one person's voice mattered. Imagine your partner calling you on the phone and only talking about their day, their accomplishments, their setbacks, and what is on their mind but never bothering to ask you about any of those things. Imagine if your partner only spoke to you once or twice a day, and when they did, it was rushed. Imagine if you were just a part of a to-do list. Imagine if during the day, no matter how many times you called, your partner didn't answer or take the time to reply to any of your messages because they were too busy.

How would that make you feel? How long do you think that relationship would last? In my opinion, it wouldn't last very long. Sadly, that's how my relationship with God looked.

In my dream, I desired to be as close to my husband as possible so I could hear his voice clearly. I drew near to him. I knew that he was the key to me being successful in navigating out of wherever I was. I was traveling in unknown territory, and he was the only lifeline that I trusted to not only guide me in the right direction but also see any potential obstacles ahead.

So, why wasn't I doing the same with God? Why wasn't my relationship with God a priority? Why wasn't drawing as close to Him as possible a priority?

Slowly, I began to realize that a relationship with God meant more than simply reading the Bible and praying. When we talk about God and getting to know Him, an emphasis should be placed on cultivating a relationship. Through a relationship, we are able to hear His voice. Through a relationship, we have unlimited access to wisdom, knowledge, and understanding. Through a relationship, we have everything we need.

We are all traveling an unknown path, it's not familiar to any of us, so why isn't our first reaction to draw near to the one who knows the direction we should go? Worry, doubt, and fear creep in when we don't know our way or have lost our way. However, when we are following and have trust in the one we are following, there is no confusion. Just like it was in my dream. The key to unlocking our greatness is a relationship.

When you establish a relationship with God, you learn His voice and can distinguish it from your own and that of the enemy. You can gain clarity as to where you are to go and where you should not. You can release fear and exchange it for faith. Though the path we are walking is unknown, it becomes less overwhelming when we know we are walking with a guide. The journey becomes easier and less overwhelming when you understand and trust that you are being led in the direction that you should go and are not alone.

The Relationship

So, how do you establish a relationship with God? The same way you would with anyone else: you make time for them.

1. Spend Time with God Daily

One of the things that my husband did and still does that makes me feel special is that he makes me a priority. So, I do the same with God. In the morning, before my feet touch the ground, I pray. After

I pray, I spend time with Him. I prioritize my time with Him above everything else.

Please know that your time with God doesn't have to be classified by a strict routine. I made the mistake of thinking that spending time with God had to look a certain way. I wasn't sure whether there was a specific amount of time that I was to spend or what I should do during the time. I was under the impression that there was a one-size-fits-all approach to cultivating a relationship with Him. But what I found was that there isn't.

The best thing that you can do is let it flow and do what feels natural to you. Think about your last close relationship, whether romantic or platonic, did you have a set of rules you followed to cultivate that relationship? Were you worried about what to do or not to do in order to get to know the person better? If I had to guess, I would guess that you went with what "felt right" and didn't put too much time into thinking about how it should go. If you wanted to call the person, you did. If you thought about that person, you didn't hesitate to let them know. If you wanted to spend time with that person, you asked. Those were all things that you probably did without worrying whether you were doing things the right way. So, why would this be any different?

Your relationship is just that, your relationship. It can look and feel however you would like it to. You may turn on a song and worship, you may pray, you may read your Bible, or you may just sit and be still. It is your time, so do what makes you feel closer to God. Your time spent doesn't have to resemble that of anyone else's. I have literally sat and had lunch with God. I told Him about my day and I took the time to listen to what, if anything, He had to say.

Whenever you spend time with God and however you spend time with Him is the right way to spend time; just remember, it's quality over quantity. You will know whether you are doing what is right for you, so make sure you tune into how you feel. If it feels right, then do it. At the end of this chapter, I will provide you with a sample framework that you can try until you establish a routine that you enjoy and can stick to.

2. Incorporate God in Everything That You Do

As I mentioned before, when my husband and I were dating, we would talk all the time. It didn't matter what time of day it was, when we thought about each other, we made it a point to call or send a text. After we became more serious, we made it a point to involve each other in the decisions we made. We treated each other like partners and made sure to check in with the other person before we made moves.

This is the same thing you can and should do with God. In whatever you do, God should be at the center of it. Regardless of whether it is big or small, He desires to be involved. Glorifying God doesn't just happen in church or during your prayer or devotion time; it can happen during any second of the day with your thoughts and actions—while you are driving, walking to work, on your lunch break, taking care of your kids, spending time with your family, anytime. No matter what you are doing, there is always an opportunity to involve God. Letting God know that you are thinking of Him is enough. Constant communication is key. Remember, God is your partner and desires to be involved in your life.

3. Express Gratitude

Have you ever had someone call you for the simple fact that they wanted to tell you they love you, they are thinking about you, or that they are thankful for you? If so, how did it make you feel? Amazing, right? So, think about this, if you felt that way, how great would God feel if you did the same to Him?

Incorporating gratitude in your life will transform not only your life but also your mindset. So often, we perceive change as this insurmountably difficult thing to do, especially when it comes to changing the way we think. When, in all actuality, it really isn't as complex as we make it out to be nor does it take extreme effort. Implementing small changes in your day can make a drastic impact.

Starting small is key, and what better way to start than to start with gratitude?

4. Be Still

This is extremely important. Often, we aren't able to hear God's voice because we haven't taken the time to slow down, be quiet, and listen. Taking time to listen shows that you not only prioritize the person but also care about what the other person thinks and feels. When you set aside time and space for God to communicate with you, He will.

The Challenge

Using what we have discussed, I challenge you, for the next thirty days, to work on cultivating and strengthening your relationship with God. If you aren't sure where to begin, here is a sample routine you can use to either establish or improve your relationship with God.

1. As soon as you wake, pray. Start with gratitude. Think about at least five things you are grateful for and thank God for them.

2. Play a worship song and either sit and listen or sing along with it.

3. Pray for God to open your eyes, ears, and heart to receive everything that you need. Ask for the ability to focus and not be distracted, ask for discernment, and ask if there is anything specific that you should read and let God know that you are readily available to listen.

4. Spend ten minutes meditating and being silent. Allow God to speak to, lead, or prompt you.

5. Read a devotional, the Bible, or something inspirational.

6. Spend five minutes meditating on what you read and allow it to be imprinted in your mind.

7. Visualize yourself having a close relationship with God where you are walking confidently in your calling, you are being led in the right

direction, and where fear, doubt, and worry no longer plague you. See yourself constantly being offered opportunities and knowing the right one to choose each and every time because you have wisdom and discernment. Visualize what you want in a relationship with God and what you are expecting to come from it. Exercise your faith and end with gratitude.

This is no more than forty-five minutes out of your day that will make a greater impact on your life than anything else will. You have and can find forty-five minutes in each day to spend with God. So do it! Start off here and eventually work to spend more time. Sprinkle the time throughout your day. Remember, whatever feels right, move in that direction. Try new ways of incorporating God in your day-to-day life. That's where He wants to be. He desires to be involved in your everyday life, so let Him in.

I didn't prioritize my time with God because I thought I didn't have time to do so. I thought being still, spending time with God, and doing the work necessary to strengthen our bond was a setback for me achieving my vision and fulfilling my calling. As I looked to my left and right, it seemed like everyone else was on the go and accomplishing the things that they wanted to; I felt that if I were to spend idle time, I would be left behind. I needed to be busy; that's what made me feel like I was accomplishing something. In my mind, I couldn't afford to spend the time necessary. But in all actuality, I couldn't afford not to.

When I started making God a priority and doing the necessary work to strengthen our bond, things slowly began to change and, honestly, are still changing because I am still on the journey. I've received direction, wisdom, and have had plenty of revelations, which have prompted me to make changes in my life. The closer I get to God, the less anxiety I feel. The more I seek Him, the more is revealed to me. The stronger our relationship becomes, the more confidence and wisdom I gain.

If there is anything that you should be doing, it is seeking God. The Bible states in Matthew 6:33, "But seek first the Kingdom of God and His righteousness, and all these things will be added to you." "All these things" includes everything you need to fulfill your purpose and walk in your calling. "All these things" includes the vision that God has shown you and the promises He has made to you. Matthew 7:7–8 states, "Ask and it will be given to you; seek and you will find; knock and the door will be opened to you. For everyone who asks receives; the one who seeks finds; and the one who knocks, the door will be opened." Seek God and continue to knock at His door. It all starts with a relationship. That one simple thing can change your entire life.

Much love on your journey.

About the Author

CHRISTINA THOMAS

Christina Thomas helps people move out of their own way and achieve their dreams in real estate and real life.

In her chapter, "Are You Listening?", Christina shares with us how she learned to listen to the divine wisdom she was receiving and incorporate it into her life. She concludes her profound chapter by challenging us to take actionable steps in order to grow our connection with God.

Christina is a licensed realtor, an investor, an attorney, a speaker, a juvenile justice reform advocate, and a co-founder of Annu Smoothie Cafe. She also broadcasts a weekly "Hour of Power" at six o'clock in the mornings on LinkedIn and YouTube to help people step out of their comfort zone, believe bigger, walk confidently in their calling

She lives in the DMV area with her family.

LinkedIn: https://www.linkedin.com/in/christinathomasesq/

SIXTEEN

Katrijn Van Oudheusden

AWAKENING THE SERVANT LEADER WITHIN

In a silent auditorium filled with hundreds of people, tears were streaming down my bare face, dropping onto clenched hands. I was more amazed at my uncharacteristic display of emotion than I was ashamed of it, even though any of us could end up on camera and in a marketing video. It was a small miracle that I was even here, considering my aversion to New Age gurus and their adoring disciples.

Yet here I was in Byron Katie's nine-day "School for The Work" program, and my carefully constructed and protected self-identity was collapsing onto itself like a house of cards. We had just returned from the morning walk meditation and were sitting quietly waiting for Katie (her full name is Byron Katie Reid) to take the stage and tell us we were all loved and okay. Through me coursed wave after wave of sorrow and compassion for the true me underneath the fake ego I had been trying to build up and improve most of my life.

Just like everyone else in the auditorium, I had spent decades learning to build an identity of outward success around a core of feared unworthiness. Wasn't I special for being scared to death of not being good enough? Apparently not. The rows upon rows of other people of all ages, from all walks of life, and from all over the planet seemed to be experiencing exactly the same thing.

I vividly remember one of the most beautiful and elegant women I'd ever seen getting behind the microphone to tell us she didn't think she could live with her lack of attractiveness. An Israeli soldier admitted to his deep cynicism about life and his place in it. And an endless sequence of seemingly successful, adapted, wonderful people spoke up about their lack of joy, meaning, and hope. They found it exquisitely difficult to be themselves. The suffering all of us now admitted to came from the endless limiting beliefs we had built up around ourselves, convincing us that we were somehow irreversibly flawed.

We spent nine full days cooped up in that hotel to identify, look at, meditate on, and question those beliefs. We questioned from morning to night, sustaining ourselves on gourmet vegetarian buffet meals and copious herbal tea. Tears and laughter were everywhere, sometimes simultaneously. I have never seen such mounds of used Kleenex. There were mind-blowing realizations and there were almost silent understandings. Everyone saw chunks of their limiting story fall away.

After the School for The Work, I saw them everywhere: unhappy insecure people pretending to be okay. I slowly realized that no human being was exempt. And I saw them all around me at the university where I worked. Lost, anxious people pretending to be knowledgeable and in control. Leaders and followers using various creative strategies to avoid being found out, afraid as they were of failing and disappointing themselves and others. The beliefs they had built around an insecure sense of self had become transparent to me. It was as though I could suddenly see right through them.

What I felt for them, to my amazement, was a strong connection and overflowing empathy. Here was my boss, a professor, and a president, literally begging to be loved and appreciated by anyone around him. And my worst colleague, transparently attempting to shore up his fragile self-worth by consistently bragging about his achievements and berating his team for their work. It was suddenly so clear that everyone was engaged in complex strategies to avoid the beliefs of unworthiness at their core.

Chestnut Trees

My awakening may have started with Byron Katie, but it most certainly didn't end there. I still felt that core of unworthiness acutely. What followed were five more years of intense spiritual examination followed by a gentler process of discovery that continues to this day.

I wanted to understand why I was so unhappy and unfulfilled and get to the very core of it. I wanted to know how to feel effortless joy in being my authentic self. Most of all, I wanted my life to have meaning, and I intuited that it would only be found by transcending the inner unworthiness and being in service to something larger than my ego. I knew I would have to continue to look deeply within to be able to do that. And so the real search was born.

At that point, work had come to feel completely pointless. I was in a state of permanent bore-out. I knew it was about me and my inner mess, not about the work itself. As an organization development professional, I was involved in change projects with company-wide scope. I had the opportunity daily to move things forward. It didn't mean much to me anymore.

To find the meaning I so craved, I would have to realize that I wasn't what I thought I was. It was clear to me that it was all about awakening to my true nature now. Intuitively, I knew the sense of unworthiness to be false, and I knew that to see that clearly would lead to the meaning I was looking for. A part of me felt guilty for becoming so involved with myself. Another part of me knew it had to be done.

I started reading spiritual literature like an obsessed woman—*A Course in Miracles*, Eckhart Tolle, *Conversations with God*, countless Buddhist and nondual authors. I even read behavioral therapy and psychology textbooks. Book after book appeared on my Kindle and was devoured. Then there were videos of teachers to watch, new insights to discover, and more enlightened masters to read about. It was a fascinating world of ideas that resonated deeply mixed with distracting words in foreign languages and frequent contradictions about what the path to awakening should look like.

My days often contained a variation of the following thought: *By the time I reach the next tree, the illusion of ego will be seen.* I would be on my daily walk home from work, four kilometers through the green town I lived in. Near the end of my route was a long avenue lined with old chestnut trees. I'd been reading once again about the illusion of self, and my mind was telling me it had understood already! Why wasn't I experiencing it though? I clearly still experienced an ego. I didn't like it, and I wanted it gone. By the next chestnut tree, I hoped. Looking back, I can laugh at "my" ridiculous wish to get rid of ego just by wanting it badly enough.

This went on for two or three years. What I never did was try any of the many practices suggested by these authors. I read all about them at home but my thoughts quickly convinced me that I had already understood what was being said and didn't need to investigate further. Sure, I dabbled a little here and there. I would stick with a form of meditation or visualization for a few days. Or I would examine some concept in my mind for a while. But it wasn't dedicated, and it certainly wasn't from an open heart. I continued to believe that the next book would "do it" for me.

My upbringing and education taught me that learning takes place through reading and thinking. Growing up in a family of academics, surrounded by books, only strengthened this cultural paradigm. Intuiting, knowing beyond thought, or allowing creativity to well up were all unacceptable means of understanding the world. I remember very clearly the instructions in school to use logical, rational arguments for everything. Even creative subjects like art were "learned" by teaching us to think about perspective, line, and form.

Like many of my current clients, I was looking for the answer in the mind, in thought. I was trying to understand it all with my thinking. But if you awaken from the self-illusion, you wake up to the thinking mind. Awakening is beyond thought and cannot be found in our heads. I made the innocent and common mistake of looking only in thought to explain and understand.

Finally, I grew too fed up to read another book. I wanted to know the truth for myself and without any doubt. I didn't want to have to remind myself by reading the next spiritual author, hoping the content would move into my being through osmosis. And so I finally, reluctantly, started to do some of the practices and exercises that spoke to me. Something in me realized I needed to look in my own experience to find the insights of what I was reading and learning. I had to embody them.

I'd like to tell you that at that moment things immediately changed: that there was some epiphany and complete enlightenment realized. The truth is less exciting, but the insights remain undoubted and lasting to this day. Mine was more of a low-key waking up. I gather it is like that for many people. There is no lightning, no angels, no singing of heavenly choirs. There's just a simple but truly unshakable knowing: yes, this is the truth. The separate, fearful, unworthy self is a construct in thought. There is only this everything. It didn't require any form of "spirituality" for me.

The Four Insights

There's an unfortunate narrative in spiritual circles that seeing our true nature is going to be a grueling, unpleasant process. Traditional Buddhists talk of it taking many lifetimes and a monastic life. The modern psychological version is that we will have to deal with every last bit of our "stuff" first, along with a deep suspicion toward anyone who claims to have understood anything about our true nature without years of effort. Or there is rhetoric about battling the ego in an almost mythical show of strength that few will be able to muster.

I find this unfortunate because I and many others have found it to be untrue and off-putting. Yes, the danger that some will bypass all spiritual work and walk around with a fake enlightened ego exists. All my reading and not practicing was one version of that. But I'm not sure an ego pretending to be awake is worse than any other ego. I believe we serve others better by encouraging them to walk this path and presenting it as clearly as possible instead of scaring them away from it. This is why I avoid the struggle rhetoric and any psycho-spiritual jargon that complicates the message unnecessarily.

Now that I guide others to see these things for a living, I have come to describe our true nature in four insights that anyone can see for themselves and lead directly to effortless and authentic servant leadership. That means these insights have a pertinent application in the corporate world where a more awake and conscious leadership is desperately needed.

The four insights are neither esoteric nor particularly difficult to see once we know how to look. We've just been trained to look in the wrong direction. Many authors call it the open secret. Every human being can wake up to their true nature. Waking up means we end up with a heart that is wide open and willing to serve first. We just can't stop it anymore. That is why the result is service.

Servant leadership is already within us as our higher or true self. We've covered up this true self with various illusions. This means we don't need to learn anything new to become servant leaders. We don't have to evolve, grow, or develop ourselves. Instead, we must rediscover and uncover what is dormant within us all. The "path" is to unsee our illusions about ourselves.

Servant leadership, expressing our true self at work, will look different for everyone. The inner nature is the same, but it will be filtered through our unique personalities and characteristics. We don't have to become the clone of Mahatma Gandhi or develop into a saint. Neither can we look to others for how to be servant leaders. We have to uncover and embody our unique version.

Insight 1: We are being lived

The first insight is that we are not managers in control of our lives, so we can stop worrying about how to succeed at living. We can let go completely and move into a natural, effortless flow, allowing life to live us, completely in sync with what is already happening.

Since birth we have been told the exact opposite. We have been trained and conditioned to believe the illusion that we are in control of our lives and must do everything we can to make life a success. Success is defined in many different ways, and we are taught very different strategies depending on the culture in which we grow up. Nevertheless, we have to control life to succeed. Seeing through this illusion results in the discovery of work as "flow". Instead of pushing, striving, and fighting for our version of reality, we move in sync with what emerges. We dance with it.

One leader I coached describes it as the biggest stress reliever of her career. She used to go into every meeting, no matter how insignificant, anxious and sweating. Her most important goal was to say exactly the right thing for the others to sway her way and give her what she wanted. It was frustrating and extremely demanding trying to control a million variables along with her behavior.

Discovering the first insight for herself led to a complete turn-around. Going into meetings completely at ease, alert but relaxed, meant that she could respond intelligently to what came up. No longer trying to force control over the situation, she was present and undistracted enough to sense what was happening as it was emerging. Meetings became her flow state, and although not everything went in her favor, she got much more out of them due to her awake dance with reality.

Insight 2: We are new in every moment

We are not the limiting stories, assumptions, or beliefs we have about ourselves. We can let the learned, conditioned, limiting ego-story be and be new in every moment, without guilt over the past or anxiety about the future. We can also easily see that others are not defined by our beliefs about them nor by their own beliefs about themselves. Our judgment of self and others wanes, and we can keep our hearts open.

Since birth we have been belief collectors. Our surroundings told us who and what we are, experience seemed to support or contradict this, and out of this medley of influences our self-narrative was constructed: I am too emotional; I should be more assertive; people can't be trusted. We swallow these thoughts and add them to our identity. Over the years, the identity shifts and evolves, but we always have a set of beliefs that constitute our ego-self.

Clients come to me with endless limiting beliefs about their leadership. The core version of all of them is some version of not being good enough. Often, this makes us believe we don't "have what it takes" to be servant leaders. We have impostor syndrome and fear we are not humble or generous enough to be in service to others. One client in particular believed he wasn't "developed" enough. He measured this for himself by the reaction of other people to his attempts at support. When he determined that they weren't helped by his service, he took it personally and gave up.

Seeing this limiting belief clearly and recognizing it as a story he had learned to tell about himself allowed him to let go of it in his work. He came to understand that serving others is an intrinsic part of his human nature and not something he needed to develop first. Interestingly, the people around him noticed that the underlying agenda of getting approval and appreciation for his service had disappeared. Noticing this, they were more open to his support. The result was a better ability in servant leadership without an ounce of self-improvement.

Insight 3: We are all connected

The apparent boundaries between people are constructed in our minds. Most of us remember our experience of boundlessness as small children before we learned to separate everything into discrete objects. There was just the seamless experience of everything appearing in our awareness. One particularly strong memory for me is of sitting in a tub of water as a small child, splashing about outside. The tub was me, the droplets in the air were me, the smell of wet concrete and the clouds in the sky: all of it was me.

We quickly learn to separate, identify, and judge according to like or dislike: this is a table; this is Aunt Mary; this is a spider (don't touch it!). We are trained to see separation and difference. We train in comparison and judgment until it is automatic and constant. Then we are surprised by our loneliness.

As leaders, we learn we need to do things "to" others, even if they are deemed entirely positive: motivate, inspire, and grow people. Yet the opposite of separation is the case: everything is one. Separation and difference are constructed in our minds. We cannot do anything to anyone else. Separation is a useful construct to navigate this world up to a point but causes unnecessary problems if we see it as the only reality.

Seeing in direct experience that the border between self and other is a construct changes everything in how you lead. You discover an unshakable connection to others. You stop thinking in self/other categories much of the time. You discover that serving others is the same as serving yourself. There's just one seamless dancing existence, and the most meaningful natural occupation is to be in service to it. This is an essential part of making servant leadership effortless.

As one client put it recently: "I see others as I see myself now. And I don't need to struggle for it. I see the obvious connection between everyone. I can't name or describe it, but I know it's there. It's become more tangible to me than the differences."

To be clear, this doesn't mean you start liking everyone or losing your boundaries. Liking is based on personality, and you don't suddenly lose yours. We're talking about something much deeper than like and dislike. You can see connection and still have boundaries. You can see connection and still get into constructive conflict. The sense of separation will not disappear unless you get some pharmacological help. But with a clearer sense of the illusion of boundaries between us, servant leadership is no longer a doing but a being. It becomes our default way of showing up in the world.

Insight 4: Leadership as service is the most meaningful work

The final insight is that the most meaningful work is leadership as service. Meaning and joy in life don't come from achieving a specific position, from acquiring wealth, or from becoming a better person. When we see we are not in control, are not limited, and are all connected, the result is naturally that we want to be what we already are: in service to life. For this, we discover we can use our unique gifts since we are living this life through our individual body–minds.

Society tells us that to make a living in this world we must continually do, act, strive, and improve. The meaningful thing to do is have a great career (or the equivalent in your culture). Our leadership ambitions are often first based on such motivations, and that's okay. Sooner or later we realize that this societal narrative is also untrue. Achieving any ambition never leads to lasting happiness; being in service does.

Seeing through the illusion of striving and achieving is a question of fully understanding the first three insights. This fourth insight then naturally and easily comes through. We now realize that transcending our self-interest and leaving our unique selves in service to a larger whole is the only thing left to "do". Our natural, authentic innate servant leadership shines through and can be expressed because we got ourselves out of the way.

Servant Leader to Servant Leaders

What happened to the crying, hand-clenching character from the School for The Work? It's been more than a decade since that day. Seeing the four insights for myself, in my own experience, without doubt, led me to finally, after many detours, focus my work completely on serving others through coaching.

Coaching servant leaders is how I live servant leadership through my unique personality and skills. It's my daily work and my spiritual practice in one. It's the most demanding and meaningful practice I have ever done, more demanding than any meditation retreat. For clients, I am present and aware continually. I must look beyond self-interest and ego continually or I can't serve in any way. I need to let the connection between us come to the foreground and not allow thought to interfere. And then I serve and lead, for as long as our coaching relationship lasts.

My message to you is that servant leadership is open to anyone ready to see through the illusions blocking access to our hearts. I wholeheartedly wish for you to discover this source of joy for yourself. My coaching supports you in this journey to the most meaningful and fulfilling work you will ever do.

About the Author

KATRIJN VAN OUDHEUSDEN

Katrijn van Oudheusden is a servant leader to servant leaders.

In her chapter she writes about her discovery of four insights that reveal our innate leadership as service, allowing it to well up effortlessly, authentically, and joyfully from its source inside ourselves.

With over twenty years of international experience as a coach, management consultant, and organization development professional, she has focused her coaching practice on guiding leaders toward these four insights, using a unique online process that applies sixteen selected insight practices from world wisdom traditions.

Katrijn has completed personal coach and nondual coach training, Byron Katie's School for The Work, as well as systemic organization development qualifications. Her coaching is based on her understanding of nondual approaches, which emphasize the unity of all existence.

Originally from Belgium, Katrijn grew up as an expat child in Bangkok, Thailand. After university and first work experience in the Netherlands, she moved to Germany in 2008. She serves leaders located all over the world in English, Dutch, and German from her home in Frankfurt.

LinkedIn: https://www.linkedin.com/in/katrijnvo/
Website: https://katrijnvanoudheusden.com/

About the Publisher

Kayleigh O'Keefe

Kayleigh Marie O'Keefe is a USA Today bestselling author and the founder and CEO of Soul Excellence Publishing, which amplifies the wisdom of conscious, courageous leaders in business.

The company's debut books—***Leading Through the Pandemic: Unconventional Wisdom from Heartfelt Leaders*** & ***Significant Women: Leaders Reveal What Matters Most***—both reached Amazon international best-seller status across key business categories. Kayleigh also works with leaders who desire more meaning—and greater impact—through her signature Soul Excellence Leadership framework.

Prior to founding the company, Kayleigh spent nearly a decade as a researcher and consultant for Fortune 500 executives with CEB (now Gartner) and as a sales and customer success leader at Snapdocs, a real estate technology company. She received her BA from Duke University and her MBA on a full scholarship from the University of San Francisco.

Kayleigh has walked over four hundred miles across two different routes of The Way of St. James pilgrimage through Spain and Portugal. After spending most of her career in Washington, DC and San Francisco, she now lives and creates by the beach in Ft. Lauderdale, FL.

Website: https://soulexcellencepublishing.com/
Website: https://kayleighokeefe.com
LinkedIn: https://www.linkedin.com/in/kayleighokeefe/
Instagram: www.instagram.com/KayleighOK_11
Email: kayleigh@kayleighokeefe.com

Made in the USA
Middletown, DE
19 November 2021

52278142R00119